TAKE THE LEAP

ANDREW MOSES

Edited by Danielle Dyal, Shauna Perez, Ireidis Landaeta and JD Kudrick.

Cover image used with permission by Epicstock Media/Shutterstock.

ISBN 978-1-7370916-0-8 (paperback)

ISBN 978-1-7370916-1-5 (ebook)

Visit the author online at:
www.andrewmoseswrites.com

CONTENTS

SPECIAL THANKS TO MY BACKERS

Mike & Kerri Wilkes

Noah Love

Brad & Marcy Riegg

Ian & Sabrina Propst-Campbell

Brian & Mireya Overcast

Keith & Lorri Moses

Mike & Vicki Abbaté

Dave & Jeanne Snodgrass

Carolyn Deemer

Juan Cortés

Alex Williams

Jordan Moses

Jordan Bright

Nat & Rachael Dunn

Matt & Maralle Moffat

Brady Johnson

BJ & Linda Herbison

Josh & Audrey Arthur

Casey & Liz Fast

Ezra & Kyleigh Dunn

Ryan & Michelle Samuelsen

Ali Santacruz

Gary & Julie Williams

Tom & Debbie Dunn

Saraí Rosas

Josh Manus

Katherine Lumanglas

Collin & Jenny Barrett

Marianne Wallace

Your Brother Forever

Josué González

Ed Darnell

Cristal Villaseñor

Kyle & Amy Kendall

Carl & Donna Kjellman

Steve & Ginny Stanley

Bob & Judy Baxter

Paul & Jennifer Tyler

INTRODUCTION

Hi, my name is Andrew.

You could say I'm a risk-taker. If there's danger, if there are high speeds, if there's a possibility of rejection, I'm there. I suppose it's in going for it that I find the wonder of living.

A few years ago, I sold my car and reduced my possessions to what I could carry on an airplane. Since I was a teenager, I have been in love with Latin America. *So, why not move there? And why not now?* I left Portland, Oregon, to go where *fútbol* and tacos reign.

Today I work at a nonprofit whose mission is to bring great education and the gospel of Christ to low-income neighborhoods. I'm a teacher, but more importantly, I'm a learner.

These days, I've learned that faith in God makes us all risk-takers. That's because Jesus's teachings are big and bold. They often run contrary to popular thinking. They might even cost you something. But faith makes us say to Him, "I'll follow You anyway."

This book is about the teachings of Christ and my friends who listened to Him. Obeying Him will take you a long way: We're going to cross cornfields on a bicycle and coastal mountains in a VW bug. We'll meet Marines and teachers and orphans. We'll see the best use of a battle-ax and how much friendship costs.

Most of all, we'll see that if you trust Christ in the sure things, you can trust Him in the unknown as well.

ONE

INTO THE CAVERNS

FOLLOWING CHRIST IS A RISK

"Lean back."

This is good advice if you're relaxing on a couch or flying in first class. But I was in neither of those places. Behind me, there was nothing but air. I was standing on the edge of a cliff.

I looked over my shoulder to see what was below. Down the rock wall, there were two other climbers at different heights. Although there was space between our ropes to create different rappelling routes, the height made them look like they all converged at the bottom.

I looked at the metal anchor lodged in the rock that my rope was hanging from. If it gave out, I'd be toast: broken feet, broken legs, broken back, there wouldn't be an unbroken part of me.

I tried not to think of that as I leaned back, letting the harness bear my body weight. I fed the rope through a mechanism and started my slow descent toward the base of the cliff.

The rock face beneath my feet was limestone, the color of bone. It was wet and glimmered in the sun. I noticed little streams of water flowing through the cracks. Beside me, a waterfall came crashing down. I was almost lost in the natural beauty of it all when it occurred to me: I hadn't seen anyone with a stretcher, right? How would they get me out of the mountains in the (hopefully unlikely) case I fell? Well, helicopters, right? --the kind that rushes you to a hospital. But I wasn't rappelling down a normal cliffside. I was entering the mouth of an underground cave system, and helicopters don't go in places like that.

I hurried up my descent a little.

When I got to the bottom, I swam through a turquoise lagoon until I reached a little beach. A group of people was waiting for me there. They were wearing yellow helmets, life jackets, and black wetsuits. We were on an excursion, exploring the caves of Nuevo León, Mexico.

Above us was the precipice I had just come down. It was a triangle of blinding light framed by the towering interior of the cavern.

The guide got our attention, and we followed him through subterranean passages. We left our only source of light behind. I could see the formations of stalagmites and stalactites for a while, but the further we went, our surroundings disappeared into the darkness. I got goosebumps--the air got heavy and cold.

"Sit down in the water. You're going to slide," the guide told me.

Before me, I could barely make out the shape of a slide. The river must have carved it into the limestone as it flowed into the depths of the cave. *I'm going to slide?* My vision couldn't pierce the darkness. *How steep was it? How high was the drop?* I didn't have a climbing rope this time. *This is a risk,* I thought.

⚡

IT'S IN THOSE MOMENTS WHEN I TAKE A LEAP THAT I FEEL THE most alive. Taking the leap has become my metaphor for trusting and seeing how things turn out. You don't always need a cliff and water; you just need something of supreme worth and a little bit of courage.

Sometimes the jump is meeting someone new:

> John was standing with two of his disciples, and he looked at Jesus as he walked by and said, "Behold, the Lamb of God!" The two disciples heard him say this, and they followed Jesus. Jesus turned and saw them following and said to them, "What are you seeking?" And they said to him, "Rabbi" (which means Teacher), "where are you staying?" He said to them, "Come and you will see." So they came and saw where he was staying, and they stayed with him that day, for it was about the tenth hour. One of the two who heard John speak and followed Jesus was Andrew, Simon Peter's brother. He first found his own brother Simon and said to him, "We have found the Messiah" (which means Christ). He brought him to Jesus. Jesus looked at him and said, "You are Simon the son of John. You shall be called Cephas" (which means Peter).
>
> The next day Jesus decided to go to Galilee. He found Philip and said to him, "Follow me." Now Philip was from Bethsaida, the city of Andrew and Peter. Philip found Nathanael and said to him, "We have found him of whom Moses in the Law and also the prophets wrote, Jesus of Nazareth, the son of Joseph." Nathanael said to him, "Can anything good come out of Nazareth?" Philip said to him, "Come and see." (John 1:35–46)

These men saw something in Jesus. Some of them were drawn to the fact that He was a rabbi, a teacher. Others realized they had found the Messiah, the long-awaited king and liberator of Israel. Still others saw in Jesus the fulfillment of prophecies from centuries ago.

What the disciples saw was enough for them to take action: they left their jobs, kissed their families goodbye, and did the only thing He'd told them to do—"Follow me." I think this is the essence of a disciple: seeing someone you admire and love, and walking in that person's steps.

Maybe you see something in Jesus. I know I have, ever since I was a kid. I know that He loves me. He saves me from the cancerous sin of my soul. I belong to His family. I know Jesus will destroy death. These are promises I build my life on.

But perhaps you aren't yet convinced of this. If you have your reservations, that doesn't irritate Jesus. He didn't tell people to just have blind faith. He said, "Come and you will see," because He was ready to earn their trust.

If you want to come and see, it all starts when you read your Bible. I recommend setting aside time regularly and enjoying it with coffee. You'll see that He is an expert teacher. If you pay attention, His teachings will surprise you. They'll get stuck in your head. You'll probably find phrases you've heard since you were a kid.

In the course of your everyday life, you'll remember these teachings. Just before you buy the newest iPhone, and in doing so plunge into debt, you'll hear a little voice saying, "Where your treasure is, there your heart will be also" (Matthew 6:21). Right as you're thinking of getting sweet revenge, the voice will say, "Blessed are the pure in heart, for they shall see God. Blessed are the peacemakers, for they shall be called sons of God" (Matthew 5:8–9).

It's as if, while you are traipsing through the woods, you follow a curve in the path, remove a branch that was blocking the way, and—behold!—God points out a waterfall that you weren't expecting. I'm convinced that Jesus is like a guide who knows all the jumps on the river, and He invites you to dive off each one.

In that moment, you will have a choice to make: you can go your own way or you can follow Him and take the leap. Many people "see" the sayings of Jesus and even enjoy the view, but they leave without doing anything about it.

Why do they do this? I guess a jump means losing control. In the air, we are at the mercy of gravity. So most people stand at the ledge, look at the drop from various angles, and ask how high they are. Maybe they need this data to make physics calculations. That's understandable because equations let you see the result without ever having to try.

"But wait," they say. They check their page again, and the numbers don't add up. Of course they want to follow Christ. What He says is nice, but it seems impossible in practice.

I won't deny it: He is a danger. He'll put your comfort at risk and your self-sufficiency too. To any master that would enslave you, be it sensuality or the love of money, He is a threat.

Jesus doesn't always guarantee the outcome. If you decide to treat your rival well because you believe "blessed are the peacemakers," your enemy might have a tearful change of heart and become your best friend. It's happened. But he might take advantage of your mercy and stab you. It's happened as well.

Standing there on the ledge, the only thing you need to calculate is this: If you trust Jesus in the sure things, do you trust Him in the unknown?

THE RIVER PULLED ME DOWN INTO THE DEPTHS OF THE cavern. Down, winding down, a free fall! Then all forward movement stopped. My life jacket pulled me to the surface of a lagoon. I swam blindly, listening to the acoustic resonance of the water moving in the blackness. After a few moments, a strand of light entered through the mouth of the cave. Rays of light—curved by the water—danced on the ceiling. It felt otherworldly. I emerged from the cave into the light of day where the air vibrated with the buzz and heat of the jungle. The other explorers and I floated together, looking at each other in smiling wonder of it all.

That day was more than I had expected, more than the photos I'd seen on Instagram, more than the reviews I had read.

You'll see the same when you follow Christ.

> Jesus saw Nathanael coming toward him and said of him, "Behold, an Israelite indeed, in whom there is no deceit!" Nathanael said to him, "How do you know me?" Jesus answered him, "Before Philip called you, when you were under the fig tree, I saw you." Nathanael answered him, "Rabbi, you are the Son of God! You are the King of Israel!" Jesus answered him, "Because I said to you, 'I saw you under the fig tree,' do you believe? *You will see greater things than these.*" (John 1:47–50, emphasis mine)

Let's go see some of those greater things, let's take the leap.

TWO

EYE FOR AN EYE, TEA FOR A TEA

HOW TO DEAL WITH UNREASONABLE PEOPLE

"Everything stops right now!" screeched Celestina, her curly hair shaking as she enunciated each syllable. Although the woman standing in the hallway of the apartment was about seventy years old, she seemed like a bull from Pamplona about to trample me. "I don't want you boiling all my water or racking up huge electric bills or leaving any more messes in my kitchen. If you want tea so badly, go to a café. But in MY house, everything stops right now!"

We all have something we'll fight for, but until the ambush that night, I didn't know that for Miss Celestina this thing was tea.

This is the story of our battle.

You've already seen how it ended, but let me tell you how it started: in my second year of college, I studied abroad in Seville, Spain. It was an opportunity to learn the Spanish language and culture. I saw myself playing soccer daily and strumming a flamenco guitar for all my new Iberian friends. And I imagined myself living with a family with two kids and a little dog.

But instead I got Celestina.

"A grandmother? But they promised me a 'host family,'" I complained to the program coordinator.

"That's right. You're living with a family. Well, technically not, but…"

His answer zigzagged like a mosquito in one rhetorical direction and then off to another. It was dizzying, but I gradually came to understand that my neighbors would be Anabela and Victoria—Celestina's daughter and granddaughter—and that was how it would be as though I were living with a family.

Celestina basically did three things each day: cleaned the house, prepared our meals, and watched television. The bathroom was immaculate. If while brushing my teeth a spatter of toothpaste landed on the mirror, or if I didn't hang my towel with the Japanese precision of origami, she would let me know.

But I couldn't complain about the food. I loved her recipe for rabbit in tomato sauce. She would also fry potatoes in olive oil and served them hot. We had bread and Nutella in the mornings and vegetables in the evenings. Honestly, the only thing missing was dessert. In three months, I didn't even have a cookie. If you know anyone with weight issues, I can attest: the Celestina diet works like a charm.

We got along well even though we weren't "like a family." Meals were our time to connect. We ate at a table so small that our two cups, plates, and silverware barely fit. It was there that she told me about the Franco dictatorship and how she and her late husband fled to Belgium during those years. She had empathy for me when I struggled with learning the language or making friends because she had gone through the same experience.

After eating, Celestina often went over to the other apartment to visit her daughter and granddaughter. Sometimes they came over to visit Celestina.

Cleaning the house, eating meals together… what was missing from the routine? Right: watching television. I didn't join her in this activity because I wanted to explore. I was abroad—come on! So I wandered on foot through the alleys and avenues, along which I saw rows of parked motor scooters. I took my university books to read on park benches in the plazas. I relished my walks.

On one afternoon walk, I found a guitar shop called Taller de Guitarras Artesanas Juan C. Cayuela. Amongst the surrounding gray storefronts, its hardwood facade attracted me. I pulled open the door, and a young man showed me their selection of instruments hanging on the walls. I asked for a paper to write down the models and prices, and when I got back home, I noticed the sheet of paper featured a quote from C. S. Lewis, a British author who inspires me in the faith. It turned out the Cayuela family were Christians! From that day on, visiting the shop became part of my routine.

One day, Juan Marcos, the employee who had become my friend, invited me to the loft above the shop. The loft resembled a living room, complete with two sofas and a coffee table. Juan Marcos told me the Cayuela family had Bible studies there. Seated on the sofa, he served me tea. I closed my eyes with each sip to take in the earthy notes my palate had never tasted. "Where did you find this tea?" I asked. He said he didn't know exactly where the shop was, so he showed me a bag with this logo: *Pasión Por El Té*.

I searched for that shop for a week (don't judge me; this was before Maps on iPhones). When I found it, the awe on my face was that of an explorer stumbling upon a pyramid in the jungle. I saw glass jars filled with leaves of every color and shape. The jars were spaced perfectly on the shelves that ran across the walls from floor to ceiling. I doubted even Celestina could organize a shop more tidily than this. I wandered through Pasión Por El Té, eyeing the description tags of the blends. The employee let me open the jars, and she even served me samples in tiny teacups. I had found El Dorado.

· · ·

ONE SUNDAY PRESENTED ITSELF AS THE DAY TO SHOW OFF MY tea. Two students from my college, Shannon and Alicia, lived next door with Anabela. I invited them to my tiny kitchen to try a blend and chat for a while. They liked the idea. All I needed was permission from Celestina. Since she would be in the living room at the other end of the house and we wouldn't bother her, naturally I expected a yes. *What's more*, I thought, *she might even offer to bake us dessert.*

"Let's see, you want to invite *people off the street* into *my* house?"

I paused before answering. I hadn't been expecting this reaction. Since Celestina had seen Shannon and Alicia at least a thousand times and knew them by name, I couldn't make sense of the term *people off the street.*

It turned out the question had been rhetorical because Celestina proceeded like a bulldozer: "No, absolutely not. My obligation is to clean the house and make your meals, not host parties for all your friends." With that, she turned around and made her way back to the recliner in the living room.

In my room, a tornado of questions swirled through my head: *What does she want? To stay alone all day? And what am I to her —nothing but a necessary annoyance to help her with expenses? Well, I couldn't care less if she sat and watched TV by herself forever.*

Reflecting on my bed, I thought of 1 Corinthians 13. It says love doesn't keep a record of wrongs, love puts up with people, it forgives, and it doesn't fail.

I wrote in my diary:

> It's incredible how Scripture reorients my thoughts. Now that I've regained my balance, I remember how Celestina got me pills when I had a cold. She invited me to see her hometown of Gerena. She helped me find a guitar teacher. If I had acted in the heat of the moment, I would have done something stupid.

The next day, I walked to a home appliance store. I searched among the Italian coffeemakers and toasters and finally found them: two glass teacups and a stainless steel thermos. *It's Celestina's house,* I told myself, *so I'll respect that.* If I couldn't have my tea in her house, I would take it with me outdoors.

And who would I like to drink tea with outdoors? The first person who came to mind was Alicia who lived next door. She accepted my invitation, so I leaped into action.

I put the aluminum pot on the stove. The spiral turned red beneath it, and little bubbles started to form. Which tea would we try: rooibos chai or vanilla espresso green tea? When I opened a bag, its spicy perfume escaped. I paused a second with the bag lifted up to my nose. Then I sunk the infusion ball into the leaves and closed it nice and full. I dropped it into the boiling pot, and the red ink of the leaves spread through the water like smoke. After a few minutes, I poured the tea into the thermos, then closed it tight and put it in my backpack.

I wanted to clean before I left. I looked for the trash can to throw the used leaves into. I opened every cabinet door in the kitchen, but it simply wasn't there. But I swear I had seen Celestina throw things away. Confused by this disappearance, I put the leaves in a glass. There was a little bit of water on the countertop and—another mystery! There were no rags in the kitchen. So I swept the water with my hand to swish it into the sink. (Later, I learned that both trash can and rag were kept in a utility patio.)

My neighbor and I walked across the bridge toward downtown. We went at a pace as relaxed as the easy flow of the river below. Lights from the streetlamps twinkled on the water. On the other side of the bridge, we walked down a street between ancient buildings whose stonework glowed in the twilight, warm like live coals. These cobblestone streets were the same ones that explorers and princes had walked, and now here we were. We stopped to listen to some street musicians and sip our tea.

You know how things rarely turn out the way you plan them? As much as you might prepare, reality seldom lives up to your expectations. But that night was spicier and sweeter than I could have imagined. I didn't want it to end, not a drop of it.

That evening, that moment with a friend, that was why I had bought the tea.

When we got back home, I wanted to run up the stairs, I was that happy. I held myself together because I was in the presence of a young lady, but that didn't stop my huge smile. I said good night to her and then opened my door. It was in that moment that from two hundred miles an hour to zero, my happiness came to a stop.

"Everything stops right now!"

LET'S SEE: I HAD FOLLOWED CELESTINA'S HOUSE RULES. I HAD spent a ton of money on the tea and utensils. I had been patient. Respectful. Even creative. And now she was throwing it all in my face!

Let's be clear about what I am about to say: I didn't yell. I raised my voice more than usual, and I said (not yelling), "You're impossible!" And I went directly to my room.

They say you should never go to sleep angry, but sometimes I don't listen to what they say. All night, my conscience had me tossing and turning in my bed. It was the kind of night when you look at the alarm clock and it reads 3:05 a.m. You try to sleep. You turn. You flip your pillow over. You open your eyes. 3:09 a.m. At long last, I heard Celestina walking down the hall at 6:45 a.m.

I worked up my courage and opened the door. I walked toward the kitchen. "Celestina..."

She pulled her head out from inside a cupboard to look at me.

"I'm sorry about last night. I shouldn't have raised my voice like I did."

She put the backside of her hand against her forehead as though fainting and, in a tone worthy of Shakespeare, responded, "In all the years that my husband was with me, he never once *yelled* at me!"

That morning, she slammed a single mug of coffee on the table and wordlessly went over to her daughter's apartment. The hum of the refrigerator kept me company as I ate breakfast. At lunchtime, with the mute aggression of a mime, she slid the food off the skillet onto the plate in front of me, and then she left the house.

I heard Celestina speaking during "siesta." Since I only heard her voice between pauses, I gathered she was on the phone. I couldn't make out the words she said because my bedroom wall muffled them, but sometimes you don't need to know the words. By the tone of her voice alone, it was unmistakable what was happening: she was gossiping about me.

That wasn't fair. Now she was armed with napalm and burning down my reputation. I figured that I'd come out of this charred to a crisp. I wondered what Jesus had to say about uneven battlefields.

In Matthew 5:38, Jesus said, "You have heard that it was said, 'An eye for an eye and a tooth for a tooth.'" This is a law that appears in the Bible and in other ancient civilizations. It's about establishing punishments that fit the crimes. If someone breaks your tooth, you don't chop off their hand; there are reasonable limits. But "eye for an eye, tooth for a tooth" became a saying. People thought it was license to inflict revenge on others. However, here's what Jesus went on to say:

But I say to you, Do not resist the one who is evil. But if anyone slaps you on the right cheek, turn to him the other also. And if anyone would sue you and take your tunic, let him have your cloak as well. And if anyone forces you to go one mile, go with him two miles. Give to the one who begs from you, and do not refuse the one who would borrow from you. (Matthew 5:39–42)

That's Jesus's tactic? To let people take advantage of me? To give them more than what they intended to rip off? You just read it, would you paraphrase it differently?

I talked with my friend Juan Marcos from the guitar shop. I asked him, "Am I way off here? Is there some unwritten Spanish rule that you don't make tea at home? Am I really making her electric bill go up when I boil a cup of water?" He assured me I wasn't crazy; it was this woman who was acting strangely. Although he didn't have a clear explanation for her combative reaction, he helped me understand I had a choice: I could fly my cause like a flag, demanding my rights, or I could give them up in order to win a totally different battle. I could keep either my tea or a friendship.

When put that way, Jesus's tactic is more than logical; it's elegant.

Back home, I opened the cupboard above the stove. I grabbed both bags of tea and took out the infusion ball, the two little cups, and finally the thermos. My arms full, I took these things to my room and put them in my suitcase under my bed. I could drink all the tea I wanted back in the United States.

TWO DAYS LATER, I FOUND OUT CELESTINA HAD IN FACT burned me to the ground through gossip. My suspicion was confirmed through an encounter with her daughter Anabela. My host had gone out on a visit, so her daughter came by. She explained that the contract stipulated a meal be prepared for me, and that was why she had come over (otherwise I think Anabela would have let me starve). I sat in the chair at the diminutive table. The both of us were quiet; all I could hear was the moving of the skillet on the stove.

"Anabela," I broke the silence. "Are we okay, you and I?"

She turned around like a tornado, her eyes just as stormy. "Oh, you! You carry around a Bible but yell at old ladies. Is everything all right? No, of course not."

A moment passed, and her words echoed in the canyon between us.

"Anabela, I already said I was sorr—"

"Said you were sorry? Yeah? What if I went out and shot someone and then said..." Her voice jumped an octave, imitating a sarcastic child, "... '*Oh, oops, I'm sorry*'?"

I considered it a moment. "Okay, it's true that words don't revive the dead. But I didn't do anything irreversible. I didn't yell at your mother, but I'm not proud of having raised my voice."

She turned her back to me again to put the spatula in the crackling food. "Don't worry about it, there's no problem," she said to close the issue.

"But, Anabela, there is a problem."

She raised her right arm. "Let's just forget about it, okay?"

One thing I know: fights don't get forgotten, and they don't fade over time.

"Anabela, do you forgive me?"

Looking at the wall, she let out a weak, "Yes."

"But do you really forgive me?"

She turned to look me in the face. "Yes, Andrew, I forgive you."

Little by little, God answered my prayers for peace in the house. Like heating a home on a cold day, the atmosphere of the house warmed up by degrees. Celestina returned my greetings. She sat with me to eat. She even showed me an album with photographs from her trips years ago. As for me, I made sure one of her three daily activities wasn't something she had to do by herself anymore: I watched the news with her in the afternoons.

One night I came home. As usual, Celestina had left me dinner. And there on the table was a slice of cake with my name on a little note beside it. It was the only dessert I ate in Spain. Although she never said the words, it was her way of saying, "Things are well between you and me."

A SKIRMISH IS PART OF A MORE EXTENSIVE WAR. ITS OUTCOME is important because it contributes to the destinies of the nations in arms. It turns out that Jesus's teachings are like that too.

> And he said to him, "You shall love the Lord your God with all your heart and with all your soul and with all your mind. This is the great and first commandment. And a second is like it: You shall love your neighbor as yourself. On these two commandments depend all the Law and the Prophets." (Matthew 22:37–40)

I didn't know it at the time, but when Jesus told us not to make them pay an eye for an eye, it fit inside a greater objective:

Love them.

THREE
MY ONE-PENNY OFFERING
GIVE YOUR BEST, EVEN IF IT'S JUST A LITTLE

And he sat down opposite the treasury and watched the people putting money into the offering box. Many rich people put in large sums. And a poor widow came and put in two small copper coins, which make a penny. And he called his disciples to him and said to them, "Truly, I say to you, this poor widow has put in more than all those who are contributing to the offering box. For they all contributed out of their abundance, but she out of her poverty has put in everything she had, all she had to live on."
Mark 12:41–44

Sometimes big sacrifices disguise themselves as small acts. Let me tell you the story about my small decision to congratulate some musicians after their concert.

It all started in my last year of high school. I got an informational packet in the mail from Cedarville University. There was a DVD inside. I leafed through pictures of the campus and statistics about who knows what. It was like all the other promotional packets flooding my mail. But when I put the DVD in, I couldn't take my eyes off the screen. I watched it again. There was a segment about HeartSong, a student-led band. They practiced together all year long and then went on tours in the summer. On top of that, they got a huge scholarship. This was for me.

The audition had its own gravity. My dreams, my plans, everything rotated in its orbit. And for a few weeks, I was a space cadet: my mind far from Planet Earth and far from the task at hand as I begged the heavens, "God, please let them accept me on the team."

The day of the audition finally came. I walked into a room to see a long table with four directors sitting up straight, with sheets of paper in front of them to write their evaluations of me. They greeted me like professionals, as if the meeting was more of a procedure than a pleasure. Then they asked me to sing my songs. They were expecting contemporary pop-rock songs, but I had secret weapons that would really dazzle them: a worship song from the nineteen-nineties and, just to flaunt my versatility, a song in the spicy Spanish style of flamenco. What's more, to show them I could help run the HeartSong blog, I'd made sure my portfolio included a letter I had written.

When it was over, the directors looked at me in that awkward silence when nobody knows what to say. I might as well have juggled and spit fire while dancing the cha-cha-cha. Can you believe it? They didn't accept me.

It was instantly clear to me: I should have made the effort to adapt myself to their repertoire, to be exactly the musician HeartSong needed. Ouch, lesson learned.

The sting to my ego would have healed, but again and again circumstances arose that opened the wound. For starters, I had signed up for a class called Worship Practicum. I called the class "How to play in a rock band." It actually was practical: we learned tips on how to perform, how to arrange a group onstage, and how to design a set of songs that flowed. My issue was that our professor also served as the director of HeartSong. And the class took place in the HeartSong practice studio! This way, every Tuesday and Thursday, I got a reminder of how pathetic a musician I was. And don't even get me started on "constructive criticism."

I became a detection dog, but I wasn't smelling out drugs —I was on the lookout for everything I didn't have now that I wasn't a member of HeartSong. One day, I saw that their studio had its own refrigerator (which my tuition kept stocked, no doubt). Another day, I thought I noticed all the musicians had changed how they dressed. *Did they get to go on a shopping spree?*

On top of all this, I had a conspiracy theory that the members of HeartSong had VIP passes to every event on campus. Like one year I couldn't play in the series of student concerts on campus because all the slots had immediately filled. And who played in the open-air shows in the plaza with tiki torches and campfires? The HeartSong kids. Who always led the music during our services on campus? The HeartSong kids. I added all this up in a mental spreadsheet.

ALRIGHT, LET'S NAME THIS: I WAS GREEN WITH ENVY.

Envy is like a pen that explodes in your backpack. It colored my academic effort. It blackened my perception of the university. My successes in the past were stained by this failure in the present. And my satisfaction in God? Unrecognizable.

One night, my friends and I went to a basketball game. I watched how the players passed the ball: dribbles between their legs, no-look behind-the-back passes. Suddenly, our Haitian player lifted off the court and slam-dunked the ball with two hands. The crowd, a sea of yellow and blue shirts and painted faces, went nuts. The air vibrated with a cheer: "Oo-ah-oo! Oo-ah-oo!" We yelled in unison, rising and falling in pitch like a siren.

But I, dumbfounded, retracted into my thoughts. I considered: *These players and I are from the same class. I'm older than some of them. How are they able to pull off these crowd-pleasing stunts?* I counted with my fingers: *They're on a team, they practice together all year long, and they have a professional coach. On a team—there you go. People can achieve greater things when they coordinate their efforts. If only I could be on a team. But instead of practicing ball handling, we would practice music. Yes! A team. Something like … like …*

I couldn't even enjoy basketball because of HeartSong.

I had turned HeartSong into the symbol of all my defeats past, present, and future. I know it wasn't fair to do so, and it wasn't logical either. But that's how envy acts.

As a consequence, praise time in our worship services became difficult for me. Each time HeartSong played, an arm-wrestling fight began in my mind. One arm was my ego, and the other was the part of me that loved God. The fight began with one side criticizing the mechanical way the singers spoke between songs; then the other side would ignore who was playing and instead affirm the lyrics we were singing. Soon I would imagine myself playing the guitar, but then turn around and give myself a sermon about how this was not about me but about adoring God. One side to the other, one side to the other. It was a struggle because you can't worship God and harbor envy at the same time. One of them has to win.

As we saw in the passage that started this chapter, the poor widow impressed Jesus. She wasn't like the rest who gave offerings from what was left over from their riches. They could give without their donations impacting their personal economy. They could approach God without having to trust Him. They could leave the holiness of His presence the same as they'd come, without having been transformed. But transformation on the inside is the point of sacrifice:

> For you will not delight in sacrifice, or I would give it;
> you will not be pleased with a burnt offering.

The sacrifices of God are a broken spirit;
a broken and contrite heart, O God, you will not
   despise. (Psalm 51:16–17)

A change of heart is what I needed as well. I couldn't keep living with this parasitic mentality.

Like the majority of big problems, it never went away on its own. But I do remember well the start of the process of getting rid of it.

It was when I decided to submit to HeartSong's leadership. For someone in a normal state of mind, this would have been a sacrifice of "two small copper coins, which make a penny," but it cost me everything in that moment. After each service, when four thousand students headed down the walkways toward the exits, I went against the current to the front. When I got to the stage, I looked the musicians in the eyes and thanked them.

To me, that gesture was water poured on a dried-out plant. With time, I absorbed more. I gave thanks to God for where He had put me, a college student, a well-loved son, a kid with the best circle of friends he could've asked for, a sinner bent toward arrogance but washed clean by Christ. The list went on and is still growing.

Envy was a sin that dominated me for a season. What I discovered is that when you reject sin, you're actually choosing God. This is an offering, and you join the poor widow in making Jesus marvel.

FOUR

HITCHHIKING ACROSS OHIO

THE FATHER IS MORE GENEROUS THAN YOU THINK

Let me open a box for you. It's cardboard, and the faded logo tells you it was for shoes decades ago. Inside there are hundreds of photographs piled up.

I pick one up by the edge so as not to leave a fingerprint. There I am at six years old, jumping on the sofa of our living room in a complete Power Ranger outfit. In my hand is a Power Ranger action figure. My mom lined up with other eager parents in the loading bay at the back of a toy store and bought it the moment the merchandise came off the truck (these action figures were highly sought-after in those days).

I take out another Polaroid in which I'm sitting with fifty other kids in our church's children's program, AWANA. Everyone is sweaty from having played in the gymnasium. There, we memorized Bible verses and ate candy as well. That's how my Sunday evenings went: I learned the story of God with humanity.

I'll grab one more. I'm in the bow of our boat. We have the accelerator on at full, and my family is skimming so fast over the water's surface that it feels like we'll lift off and fly. There on the lake, my dad taught me how to jump off cliffs and cross under our boat while swimming. If I have any bravery today, it's because he awoke it in me.

Summing up my childhood, I'd say my parents were the very definition of love, God was the definition of kindness, and life was an adventure.

But something happens as the years go by. With your first love, you realize relationships are fragile. You learn at school that success is more elusive than you thought. After an audition or two (like mine with HeartSong!), you realize you don't always get chosen. And eventually, at least in my case, it becomes difficult to get your hopes up. Everything you once thought was so sure now comes with a question mark at the end.

I think this is one of the reasons Jesus tells us to become like children. He wants us to go back to the simplicity of childhood, but this time to let it be a mature simplicity—a simplicity that doesn't forget God's heart. One way to do this is by believing God when He says He is generous like a good father.

> Or which one of you, if his son asks him for bread, will give him a stone? Or if he asks for a fish, will give him a serpent? If you then, who are evil, know how to give good gifts to your children, how much more will your Father who is in heaven give good things to those who ask him! (Matthew 7:9–11)

When I have to become like a child again, there is a story I always remember.

My parents gave me a wide range when I was growing up, but there was no freedom like getting on a bike. I pedaled that thing in a frenzy of delight. I could go somewhere without my

parents having to take me there! I explored all the way downtown to our plaza to play chess with the old Russian men. I
moved my pieces in the smoke of their cigars. I visited a shop
that specialized in fine guitars, always dreaming of buying one
someday. With the bike's handlebars in my grasp, the day was
mine!

I went to college in Cedarville, Ohio, a thirty-five-hour
drive by car (or nine days on a bike). So far away from my
parents, I realized every day was mine. And I had colossal
plans.

One of them was to travel sixty-three miles to see my
favorite band Big Daddy Weave. I tried to convince my new
friends, especially the ones who had vehicles, to come with me
to the concert. I put my best bait on the hook: we were going
to meet the band behind the curtains, VIP style. I had talked
with the event organizer and arranged for us to be volunteers.
I could see it all: T-shirts with *STAFF* printed on them,
pictures with the band. We'd chat with them even if it was
only for a few minutes. But we'd come back to college with
posters, CDs, and stories to tell!

To my surprise, the idea wasn't colossal enough. I didn't
convince anyone. As a consequence, I didn't have a car to get
there.

This was just a chance to dream bigger! I'd make the
journey on my bike.

It looked like a pack mule. The saddlebags on my bike
were stuffed with water bottles, a box of cereal, extra bike
parts, and a jacket. I tied my sleeping bag on top because I
would be traveling two days and camping in a cornfield
overnight. I put in my earbuds and blasted Carlos Santana.
Ready.

The smooth asphalt passed under my wheels easily. The
wind mussed up my hair. I breathed in the sweet smell of grass

and streams. The bike trail crossed the countryside and ran through a living tunnel made of intertwined treetops. Sunbeams filtered through the leaves.

I saw a house here and there separated by extensive cornfields. As I went on, the fields shrunk into yards. House by house, the landscape turned into a suburb.

Then—*boom!*—the bike trail intersected with an avenue and didn't continue. It disappeared. This wasn't supposed to be the end of the bike trail. I turned around in a complete circle, scanning my new urban environment. Where did the trail pick up again? I took out my map of Ohio's bike trails to find my bearings. It was easy to unfold because I'd printed off the map on an eight-and-a-half-by-eleven-inch sheet of paper. According to the map, this city was a black pixel connected to other black pixels by red lines. These red lines should have been bike trails. I blinked. This wasn't going to help me at all. I looked to the heavens and shouted out, "God, help me, please!"

I began to knock on doors so a local could tell me where I was. Maybe they saw me at a distance and were grossed out by my sweaty shirt, or maybe they smelled me from inside their houses, but whatever it was, no one opened their door. So I continued into the city believing God was going to guide me.

He did it in the form of a man pedaling his bike through a park. From afar, I could see his gnarly tattoo, muscly arms, and shaved head. Could he belong to a bicycle gang? But from a different angle, I saw that behind him was another seat, and in it—a smiling baby! How bad could he be?

He turned out not to be bad at all. He stopped, and I asked for directions to Greenville. The town didn't ring any bells for him. I showed it to him on my map, to which he replied, "Dude, you need a real map." We went to buy one at a 7-Eleven. On the way, we introduced ourselves. His name was Jason, and his son was Gabriel.

Outside the convenience store, we opened up the enormous three-by-three-foot map of Ohio I had just bought. I pointed to Greenville with my index finger.

"There? That's where you want to go?"

"Yep. There."

"Are you aware you're going to have to go through downtown Dayton? Drug pushers and gangs roam there. The police don't even go into some of those neighborhoods."

I didn't know if this was a question or a talking-to.

Jason went on, "You, a white kid on a bike, are going to go through there at night? I just moved out of there. You're gonna get shot, I promise ya."

The two of us went silent for a moment. His squinted eyes darted this way and that. I could see he was thinking about what to say.

"Look, I wasn't going to do anything tonight. I can give you a ride to Greenville in my car."

I know. I shouldn't have gotten into a car with a stranger. Honestly, that hadn't been part of my master plan, remember? But, well, here went nothing.

Over the hour-and-a-half ride, I listened to and learned a lot about Jason. The conversation covered carpentry, his profession, his son, and also his faith.

The miles went by fast, and before I realized it, we had arrived at the Greenville Fairgrounds. Jason and I said goodbye in the light of his car's front beams. Just before starting his engine, he opened his trunk and took out a windbreaker jacket. "It's cold, Andrew. This is for you." With this and a hug, my new friend drove away.

I walked with my bike through the grassy fields of the fairgrounds looking for a place to unroll my sleeping bag. I saw what looked like a fleet of parked campers and changed direction to explore the area.

A couple walked up to me. "Hello! Good evening," they said. It was a husband and wife with well-combed silver hair. As I walked closer, I could see the wrinkles near their eyes, the kind only years of smiling leave. We stopped and talked for a while. They were warm, and I felt like they could have been my grandparents. They were staying there with their friends for a weekend escape in their RVs.

Just when I was about to say good night and look for a place to sleep under the stars, they invited me to sleep on their sofa. I hadn't imagined spending the night like that, but how could I reject their hospitality?

My concert duties started at seven in the morning. All the volunteers gathered together and received instructions for the day. I was slightly disappointed we didn't get *STAFF* T-shirts, but too excited for the arrival of my favorite band to let it get to me. Soon we were setting up speakers the size of refrigerators, unfolding chairs for the audience, and hanging banners.

In the distance, I heard a diesel motor change gears. At the base of a dust cloud rising from the gravel road, I saw an RV approaching. Painted in big letters on the side was *Big Daddy Weave*. My heart beat a little faster.

The first one out of the bus was the audio technician. He called us to help him unload equipment. He didn't have to ask me twice! He directed us like a Marine sergeant: "You, grab this and take it over there. You, grab that...." I got to carry Jay Weaver's bass!

Finally, the group came out and got acquainted with the concert venue. Seeing as how I'd finished my tasks, I thought, *Why not meet the band?* I walked up to Mike Weaver, the leader, and Jay, his brother. I introduced myself timidly, but their smiles were inviting. As they tuned their instruments, I explained to them how I had arrived the previous night. After that, they went to a pavilion to have lunch. I didn't have anything to do, so I went to the pavilion as well! Mike introduced me to the band and their crew. I almost died of happiness.

After this, they set up the merchandise booth. I helped Jeff, the drummer. We rolled a black box into place. It was about a yard high, wide, and deep. Jeff opened it up, and inside were panels, little doors, and hinges. It worked like a Transformer. Finally, we saw a merchandise booth complete with shelves, drawers, a counter, and a register. For the next half hour, as we folded T-shirts, Jeff talked with us, telling us about his three-year-old girl and another baby on the way.

When all of the merchandise was folded and arranged, I wondered what I was going to do in the hours before the concert. I saw the band heading toward a fifteen-passenger van. Where were they going? Another volunteer explained they were going to a hotel to freshen up before the big show.

Five minutes later, Big Daddy Weave, two volunteers and I were in the van heading to the hotel. The volunteers and I had lunch at a Tex-Mex restaurant while the musicians took showers. Soon, the band was ready, and we got back in the van to return to the fairgrounds.

It was in this moment that I heard them mention the city of Dayton. I gathered all the confidence I had and said, "Hey, I, uh, heard that… well, I think I understood that…" It took me a while, but I finally connected the words to ask them if they were going to Dayton after the show.

"Okay, you are then? That's crazy because I live right by Dayton! Could you take me there? … Yeah, with you. … Yeah, in your tour bus."

They weren't sure since they would be leaving me in the big city at night (the city where Jason said I'd get shot). The unresolved question hovered over me like my personal rain cloud as we continued to the fairgrounds.

The van arrived, and a few hours later, I was behind the stage again. The concert moved me like no other had before. I saw their guitar strums, their solos and riffs, everything—from behind the stage! With my head at the height of Big Daddy Weave's shoes, I saw the faces of the audience bathed in the surreal colors of the lighting. But the thing that gave me goosebumps was to hear thousands of voices singing in unison and worshipping God.

My reverie was interrupted by a finger touching my shoulder. It was the tour bus driver, Steve. He had heard about my dilemma and told me if my bicycle fit in the trailer, I could ride with them back to Dayton!

I was partially relieved but couldn't ignore that phrase "if your bicycle fits." God reminded me how He had already provided for me up to that point, and how He would provide for my return. After the event, the audio technician came out to direct us volunteers in loading up the equipment trailer. He knew exactly where all the pieces went, organizing them like he was playing a 3-D game of *Tetris*. The trailer filled up more and more. I could feel my heart drop in my stomach when I saw the boxes reach the door frame. I began to consider my options. I could go back home on my bike; that had been my original plan, after all. I could sleep in a nearby cornfield and start my odyssey home at sunrise.

"Okay, and finally," the voice of the roadie brought me back to reality, "pass me that bike." He managed to slide it on its side on top of everything!

Have you ever wondered what a band does on their tour bus? Let me tell you! We sat on sofas eating wings and celery. An episode of a show was playing in the background, but we weren't even watching it because the chatter was good. I had so many questions for them! Mike explained what each member of the band did offstage. It sounded like a startup business.

I've been around plenty of popular kids over the years. Honestly, they make me feel uncomfortable. But the guys in Big Daddy Weave were not cool kids at all. Somehow even though they were rock stars, they were down-to-earth and friendly. They made me feel welcome.

The darkness of the fields we drove through was soon broken up by the glint of amber through our windows. We'd arrived at the city, lit by streetlights.

Before they went into the hotel, I took a picture with the group. My classmates were *not* going to believe this. Then I loaded up my pack-mule bike and said goodbye to my new friends.

While I was pedaling away, I looked for a gas station, figuring someone there could help me locate myself on my mega map. I saw one two blocks away from the hotel. But when I got there, I didn't see anyone; it was one of those self-service stations. I rode in a slow circle, looking in every direction. *Any stations over there? No. … There?*

From the distance, I heard a shout. I stopped pedaling and listened. "Andrew!" That was definitely my name. I doubled back for the hotel. Behold, Mike Weaver called to me again and said, "Hey, man. We didn't want to leave you all alone out there. We have an extra bed in one of the rooms if you want to crash here."

Of course I did! I stayed in a room with Jay, the bassist. The entirety of a queen-size bed was all mine! When I woke up, the room was empty. They had left at 4:30 a.m. but said I could stay as long as I wanted. I eventually left the room to have breakfast in the hotel diner: pancakes, bacon, eggs, fruit, and coffee, all for free!

I got on my bicycle with my tummy full and heart happy. On the bike trail rolling past a wall of cornstalks, I reflected: from beginning to end, none of my adventure had turned out according to my plan. It had followed the plan of Someone whose ideas are much more colossal than mine:

What no eye has seen, nor ear heard,
nor the heart of man imagined,
what God has prepared for those who love him (1
    Corinthians 2:9)

GOD IS STILL THE SAME GENEROUS FATHER. HE DELIGHTS IN giving you good gifts. Some of them you open now on this side of eternity, but these don't compare with those to come.

The problem is sometimes you forget these gifts you've been given. You have to fight to keep your perspective, and that's why God gave each of us a photo album. Yours might be a physical book, but we all have one printed in our hearts. On rainy days, take yours out. Remember what God has done for you, and become like a child again.

FIVE

IF YOUR EYE CAUSES YOU TO SIN

ON REMOVAL, LUCIDITY, AND CONCENTRATION

There is a place where manliness reigns. It's found in the arid foothills of California. A cloud of dust rises among the desert bushes as dozens of running men come into view. "Fashionable" they are not. They are wearing identical shorts, shirts, socks, and shoes—the same clothes right down to their boxers.

One of the runners shouts, "We are mo-ti-va-ted." And in a rough chorus, the rest chant back, "WE ARE MO-TI-VA-TED." To the beat of their steps, the phrases ring out:

"We are de-di-ca-ted."
   "WE ARE DE-DI-CA-TED."
   "A-ha!"
   "A-HA!"
   "Ya-ha!"
   "YA-HA!"

With each call and response, the testosterone level goes up. "Everywhere we go ... people want to know ... who we are...."

And who are they? They are the few, the proud. They

wear the same uniform as the heroes of old. They are the Marines of the United States of America.

These recruits happily strip away the comforts of civilian life, and I suspect they do it to awaken the alpha male within. They come to run, to yell, and to howl at the moon.

And that is precisely what they do. Their superiors deprive them of sleep and food; they push them beyond their limits. The recruits march forty-eight miles loaded down with rifles and forty-five-pound backpacks. They drag themselves under barbwire and climb over obstacles.

But when they lie on their bunks after the day's activities, they never wonder what they're made of. They know it. And that's the point of today's story. Some of the best things in life only come when you remove the lesser things.

LIVING IN A GIANT MAN-CAVE IS GREAT UNTIL… WELL, UNTIL you realize something is missing. It's just—let's be honest—there is a yearning in masculinity, an impulse for more than just blowing things up. On a military base, there are no glossy red lips and none of those shapely curves. As much as you like the smell of diesel, it's nothing like the perfume of a woman.

So, what are these warriors supposed to do? What should a man do in such a situation?

That question weighed heavily on the mind of my friend Josh while he was sitting on his bunk in the barracks. Normally, the barracks is where Marines compare their muscles and tattoos, but on the weekends, it's where they plan their attack—their attack on the bars, I mean. Weekends, to them, were created for two things: alcohol and women.

The other Marines invited Josh to a strip club. Since this didn't fit in with his morality, Josh turned down the offer in a diplomatic way. But Marines aren't diplomats, they're invaders, so they insisted. But Josh's "no" remained a "no."

The other Marines' insistence turned into reproach: "Do you think you're better than us?"

It didn't help that Josh was injured. In an exercise, a tractor tire had fallen on his knee, and those four hundred pounds of rubber had torn a ligament. On doctor's orders, Josh had to sit by as his fellow men sweat through their exercises.

Now, not far from where Josh sat on his bunk, they murmured among themselves. Finally, the news broke: Josh was a Christian.

After that, these Marines began flying in slow circles above Josh whenever they could—vultures waiting for him to fall. Every afternoon after work, they gathered around him to ask "gotcha" questions about the Bible. You know, the kind designed to make you look like a fool. They continued pressing him to go with them to the strip club. Whether by hypocrisy or intellectual weakness, they were sure Josh's faith would collapse.

THERE IS ANOTHER MAN WHO RESISTED THE INFLUENCE OF THE majority. His name was Dietrich Bonhoeffer. This German pastor stayed on his feet amid the societal storm that was the Nazi Party. Bonhoeffer not only organized a German resistance, but he also took part in the Operation Valkyrie assassination attempt against Hitler.

Dietrich said the following about sexual temptation:

> The essence of chastity is not the suppression of lust, but the total orientation of one's life towards a goal. Without such a goal, chastity is bound to become ridiculous. Chastity is [the vital component] of lucidity and concentration.[1]

Sexual immorality, then, is a detour. With so many back

roads and stops along the way, some people never make it to their destination.

Ever since I've known Josh, one of his goals has been a solid marriage. He dreamed about intertwining his spirit and body with that of his spouse. They would knit together a life. His goal was embodied by those ancient words of God: *"the two shall become one flesh"* (Matthew 19:5).

But sexual sins impede our capacity to form human bonds because they are pleasure without promise, just two individuals who stay together as long as it feels good. And then one individual leaves. When this is someone's experience of "love," they have no reason to think the next person won't leave them too. The following words become hollow: "From this day forward, for better, for worse, for richer, for poorer, in sickness and in health, until death do us part."

Another one of Josh's desires, like that of any red-blooded male, was ample satisfaction in his future wife. And he was sure God wanted that for him too.

> Let your fountain be blessed,
> and rejoice in the wife of your youth,
> a lovely deer, a graceful doe.
> Let her breasts fill you at all times with delight;
> be intoxicated always in her love. (Proverbs 5:18–19)

"Be intoxicated always in her love." Ha! Who said God frowns at seduction? And that wasn't even from the Song of Songs.

But sexual immorality diminishes precisely that: conjugal enjoyment. Biologists have a term called "neural plasticity," which refers to the brain's capacity to change. Change happens when you learn something—for example, a language —but it also happens when you watch pornography. Your brain gets rewired.[2] So your expectations for love and intimacy and your preferences all start to change. On top of that, the law of diminishing returns takes effect: You lose sensitivity to your vice, and you need more and more of it to feel the pleasure you had experienced before.[3] This is the same trap people fall into with narcotic drugs.

When the Marines invited Josh to the clubs, it wasn't a question of going out for one night; Josh contemplated the life he yearned to build. And when what's at stake is your life, you need to be radical. Jesus offers the only solution:

> You have heard that it was said, "You shall not commit adultery." But I say to you that everyone who looks at a woman with lustful intent has already committed adultery with her in his heart. If your right eye causes you to sin, tear it out and throw it away. For it is better that you lose one of your members than that your whole body be thrown into hell. (Matthew 5:27–29)

Josh knew something about eyes and hell. He told me recently that at the age of thirteen, he'd had an encounter with God in which God gave Josh a vision of a fork in the road. The path diverged in opposite directions. God told Josh that he could either continue down the path of lust, captivated by pornography, and let it take him far away, or he could put his trust in God. If my friend chose the second path, God promised He would lead Josh out.

As his friend, I could see up close what Josh chose. Over the years we spent together in high school and college, he fought to keep himself free from sinning with his eyes. When he fell, we would pray together.

One time, Josh stayed the course with God in a violent way. He left his bedroom, teeth gritted, angry with himself because he had just looked at things he wasn't proud of. He marched directly to the parking lot behind his house. He was carrying a tablet he had just bought. Suddenly, the screen was in the air—he threw it. When its upward velocity slowed and it began to fall, you could hear the stout whistle of the blade of a battle ax coursing through the air. Josh smashed that thing with all his might! The impact of iron against glass sent fragments of the device flying everywhere.

I love that Josh took the leap to do this! Jesus told us to take out and throw away what causes us to sin, and my friend did it with a battle ax! Of course he used a battle ax—he has Viking blood coursing through his veins! The difference between believing *in* God and *believing* God is that the first one just nods its head while the second grabs iron and goes to work. Josh didn't care about how much he had paid for this tablet. He didn't care about the legitimate usefulness he was going to lose. He cared about his soul.

ONE FRIDAY NIGHT, JOSH WAS LEANING BACK IN A CHAIR outside the Marine barracks. The sun was disappearing slowly behind the red maples. With the chores of the day done, he could sit and enjoy the warm summer breeze. He took a sip of a cold drink. Inside, the Marines were telling manly stories in small groups, busting up in laughter every once in a while.

Around this time, Josh's friend Eddy came by. He stumbled toward Josh and sat beside him. The conversation skipped all the superficial things we usually talk about like sports or the weather, and went directly to what was really on Eddy's mind. By the way he slurred his words, Josh could tell he was drunk. Eddy aired out his theories about existence and the universe. They weren't orthodox, you might say, but Josh heard him out. When Eddy asked him his opinion, Josh shared what the Bible said about the topic.

Eddy parried away the comment as if it were a sword fight: "Yeah, but I believe *this*."

Josh noticed his defensiveness. "Eddy, I'm not trying to change your mind. I just want you to know what God says about it."

And that's how the conversation continued: Eddy spilled

his guts, and Josh listened, sharing the biblical perspective every once in a while.

The next day, Josh was getting ready to leave the base when, from a distance, Eddy saw him. He stood up and spoke to everyone seated around him, "Hey! That dude Josh! If you guys ever need to talk about serious s***, talk with him. He's a good guy!" He told everyone about how much he'd liked their conversation the night before.

The Marines in his platoon had probably never heard about the time Josh took a battle ax to his tablet, but it's hard for "the total orientation of one's life towards a goal" to go by unnoticed. Starting with Eddy, his fellow men little by little realized Josh's genuineness.

This changed the kind of questions they asked him every afternoon. The questions that had once been traps became sincere. Many of these guys had fragments of information or ideas they had heard about God and the Bible, and they wanted to find out more. Others poured out their life stories for Josh to hear. Maybe God had a word for them too.

If you know the verse about tearing out your eye, you may have noticed there's one part I have yet to talk about. Jesus didn't only ask us to take out and throw away our eyes, as if lust were the only sin that mattered to God. He asked more of us:

> And if your right hand causes you to sin, cut it off and throw it away. For it is better that you lose one of your members than that your whole body go into hell. (Matthew 5:30)

If amputation sounds extreme, how would you classify hell? But before you go to those surgical lengths, why not first remove the other things that cause you to sin? Stop going to that place that entraps you. Unplug the music that seduces you. Stop running with the people who influence you for ill. Cancel your cable or Wi-Fi. Take an ax to your tablet. Do whatever it takes.

YOU REMOVE SIN FROM YOUR LIFE BECAUSE THE CONSEQUENCES are real. But the other side of that coin is that you are saying yes to what God has for you. This is what He had prepared for my friend:

Josh's knee recuperated with treatment. Back to training with his fellow Marines, he rose to prominence. He soon got promoted to a new position with a new team, but Eddy and the men of his first squad would never forget Josh because he had become perhaps the only pastor they would follow.

In those days, Josh met his wife. I will never forget seeing them standing among hundreds of paper lanterns hanging from oak trees, Josh in his Marine dress blues and she radiant in white. He loved her with a heart undivided. And this was my wish for my friend: *"Be intoxicated always in her love."*

SIX

THE SHARPENED EDGE

LOVE WOUNDS YOU

I spent my childhood climbing trees. From the heights, I did reconnaissance like a little spy. From time to time, I would close my eyes and confuse the wind in the leaves with the roar of the ocean. There are trees so towering that walking through them feels solemn, as if you were in a cathedral.

Walking with certain people has the same effect:

> The righteous flourish like the palm tree
> and grow like a cedar in Lebanon.
> They are planted in the house of the LORD;
> they flourish in the courts of our God.
> They still bear fruit in old age;
> they are ever full of sap and green,
> to declare that the LORD is upright;
> he is my rock, and there is no unrighteousness in him.
> (Psalm 92:12–15)

One of the tree-sized people in my life is Josh, who you met in the last chapter. We became friends in junior high when we were still little sprouts. The sun was setting late that summer night. I was playing third base on my neighborhood baseball team. Everything was going as expected: the loud-mouth cheers from the dugout, the dusty air, and the crack of the bat. But then I recognized the next batter as he walked up to home plate: it was Josh from my class at school. After the game, we stayed awhile and talked. We got along well, and soon we were spending all our free time together.

I don't know what we would have done if we hadn't found each other. Whatever that combination of ingredients was that made a kid popular, we didn't have it. Drawing *Spider-Man* comics wasn't considered cool then, and neither were our Rollerblades. We had long, unkempt hair like Frodo Baggins, but way less photogenic. Josh wore glasses. Nowadays there are hipster glasses, vintage glasses, aviator glasses, sexy librarian glasses, but I think Josh bought his in the nerd section.

Nonetheless, prescription eyewear didn't keep him off the playing field. He went out with all the rest of the guys. Josh was easy to spot because among all the nonstarters standing on the sideline, he was the shortest. In the locker room among young guys changing and slamming lockers, he could never get in on the other players' humor. Their jokes made him wince. What they said about girls, well, Josh thought you weren't supposed to say things like that.

In this way, we weren't at the epicenter of anything at school, and at lunchtime, we sat in the leftover places at the margins of the cafeteria.

JOSH TRIED HARD AT SPORTS. I REMEMBER WATCHING HIM ONE day in spring while I was running with the track team. In high school, I had traded my hat and mitt for shorts and spikes, but Josh kept with baseball. I watched the field next to our track. Most of the ballplayers were jogging lazily and joking around, but Josh ran with ferocity. He was yards ahead and separating from the pack. *Man! This year, he's going to be the king of the diamond,* I thought. In the locker room after practice, I saw my friend sitting on the bench, hunched over. The coaches wouldn't even give him a chance.

In spite of it all, his will didn't break. He followed a regimen of exercise: he ran, he lifted weights, and he did pushups before sleeping—four sets of fifty, to be exact. Josh figured he hadn't chosen his size-small skeleton, but he could load it with muscle.

Months went by, and the cold nights of autumn meant football. Many men look back and think of their years of "Friday night lights" as the best days of their lives. They burst onto the field to the riot of the marching band and cheerleaders. Playing before hundreds of fans was the closest thing to stardom they'd ever have.

Josh, however, would never appear with the starters in photographs, much less at their after-parties. But off-camera, my friend kept putting in the effort.

THIS WAS A STRANGE START FOR A GUY WHO, IN MY OPINION, now eclipses everyone in our class. Paradoxically, this is how the best things make their start: they are clumsy and arduous. And that includes, if you don't mind me talking about botany again, the tree that is the pride of Michoacán, Mexico: the avocado tree.

Avocados are the fruit that crown Mexican cuisine. They put creamy salsas on their tacos and slices of green on their tostadas. And who hasn't tried their famous guacamole? People from Michoacán also share the love: you can find their avocados on tables around the planet.

Recently, I learned something about the avocado tree. I'd always thought if you buried the seed, roots would sprout and a plant would grow. I pictured the little plant getting enough rain and sun, and becoming the tree that populates the groves of my state. Against common logic, it develops in another way altogether: the beginning of its greatness is a machete. The avocado tree receives deep cuts to its vascular tissue. Literally, to its heart.

After graduating high school, piercing questions cut through Josh's heart.

He went to college to study biblical theology. He had and still has a heart for the youth. Many solid men today were mentored by Josh in their younger days. And this casual practice is what Josh wanted to dedicate his life to: being a pastor. The thing was, his major required four years of classes, but his savings only lasted him two. With no other choice, he quit studying to work at a steel fabrication workshop.

He went to work at five in the morning to sweep and sweep and sweep some more. Apparently, the cutting of steel leaves behind an abundance of metallic filaments on the floor. Josh was a novice in the workshop, so in the eyes of his more experienced workmates, he was only a little more important than the dust he swept. The journeymen or masters would never talk to an apprentice. As a result, Josh worked alone among the machines and welding sparks.

The cold and the silence of the warehouse created a vacuum—a vacuum his thoughts filled up. He felt stagnant. Love? Only disappointments to lament. Money? He was starting over from scratch. The future? While all his friends were taking off in their careers and starting to fly, Josh stared at the floor with his broom in hand. He began to question: *Where is my life heading? Where are You, God?*

Here is where it's tempting to give up. And if you do, your dreams don't grow much larger than a trip for vacations and your happiness not much more than a six-pack and the weekend. Meanwhile, angst smolders under the surface. And God? You leave Him behind with the other artifacts of your childhood.

Josh felt dizzy, yes, with a metaphorical black eye as well, but he would keep fighting. What he needed was a trainer in his corner, someone to encourage him. He found it in an older married couple in his church. They had the gray hair of age but the vivaciousness of youth. They didn't give him Gatorade, but they did invite him to their house for tea and cookies. There, with all the authority of having lived three times Josh's years, they affirmed that all this was happening for a reason. They counseled Josh to do his part by seeking Christ in prayer and by treasuring His words. Then he should wait for God to do His part; God would bring about the changes.

The advice Josh's spiritual grandparents gave him was similar to what Jesus said one time:

> I am the true vine, and my Father is the vinedresser. Every branch in me that does not bear fruit he takes away, and every branch that does bear fruit he prunes, that it may bear more fruit. Already you are clean because of the word that I have spoken to you. Abide in me, and I in you. As the branch cannot bear fruit by itself, unless it abides in the vine, neither can you, unless you abide in me. (John 15:1–4)

At the time of the cut, when the pain is acute, you can interpret the situation in two ways. One is that God doesn't love you. He doesn't care about your loneliness, and that's why He lets the ones you hold dear pass away. Your first, second, and third attempts at a career weren't successful because your dreams don't matter to God. That person you thought the world of rejected you because it was actually God who had set you aside. And the list goes on.

The second way to interpret a cut is that God loves you so much He will do everything it takes for you to produce fruit. There may be things that are working for you, things that are growing, but God comes and prunes them away. Gardeners say if a branch has a lot of leaves and buds, these use up the vitality of the plant. They don't leave much for the fruit. Fruit is what refreshes others, but some things that grow in your life don't feed anything but your ego.

At the time of the cut, I generally don't comprehend what's happening. There are times when I don't know for sure if God is doing something or if the situation is just the result of bad decisions. But I firmly grab hold of the truth that this cut fits into God's purpose, the God who is for my good. Believing Him, sometimes with clenched teeth, I can deal with the pain. I can do the one thing Jesus asks of us: "abide in me."

Josh chose to interpret his situation the second way. He wanted God in his thoughts, and he had a lot of time in the workshop to think. He was in constant prayer while he swept. The silence allowed him to commit passages of Scripture to memory.

I had graduated college and was back in Portland during this time. Josh and I talked a lot, above all when we went climbing at a rock gym. The tone of our conversations, which at one point had been depressing, lifted over a period of months. Finally, when I asked him about his job, he told me about his mornings and sounded like someone savoring fine wine. He found in a steel workshop what he had looked for in college: not theological treatises, but God Himself.

THE AVOCADO TREE YOU SEE IN THE ORCHARDS OF Michoacán is a hybrid. The species of avocado with strong roots, they cut at the waist. They don't need more than its trunk because the fruit it produces is tasteless. Another species that produces robust avocados, they tear off its branches. They can't let it grow because its trunk is so feeble, it will collapse in strong winds. And so they graft the one onto the other.

There's no other way. It seems God wanted to graft into Josh lush branches that would flourish: humility and perseverance. These are qualities we aren't born with, but qualities found in the hearts of true leaders. And that is what he became.

Today, Josh is no floor sweeper. He can be found in latitudes around the world, maybe jumping from an airplane or executing an amphibious infiltration. We can't know because it's classified information. My friend is one of the elite operators of the special forces of the United States. He can evade an enemy army, understand their language, drop ordnance on their position from the sky, and clear buildings room by room in his search for them. If he gets his eyes on them, his aim is very, very good.

I HAVE PICTURES ON MY CELL PHONE OF JOSH AND ME AT thirteen years of age and others of us at thirty. I love to show off the before-and-after of my friend. That's because a lot of times I find myself in a *before* phase waiting for the *after*.

Maybe you do too. Remember, though, these cuts aren't random; they are part of the pruning process. At the handle of the machete is the hand of a God who loves you. He's grafting beautiful things into you.

Each time we obey Jesus, we do it in faith, but the question today is, will you trust Him when He hurts you?

SEVEN
PRAY LIKE YOU MEAN IT
GOD HEARS THE PERSISTENT

And he told them a parable to the effect that they ought always to pray and not lose heart. He said, "In a certain city there was a judge who neither feared God nor respected man. And there was a widow in that city who kept coming to him and saying, 'Give me justice against my adversary.' For a while he refused, but afterward he said to himself, 'Though I neither fear God nor respect man, yet because this widow keeps bothering me, I will give her justice, so that she will not beat me down by her continual coming.'" And the Lord said, "Hear what the unrighteous judge says. And will not God give justice to his elect, who cry to him day and night? Will he delay long over them? I tell you, he will give justice to them speedily. Nevertheless, when the Son of Man comes, will he find faith on earth?"
Luke 18:1–8

Have you ever met a woman like this widow Jesus spoke of? Have you met a five-foot-tall force of nature like this? If somebody gets between this mama bear and her cubs, they'd better watch out!

When you adopt the widow's mindset, your prayer life escalates. Maybe you've heard prayers as dry as old bread, but the widow's are robust. It's not about reciting words; it's about crying to Him. And it isn't a Sunday thing; it's a grit thing. You "cry to Him day and night."

And what does God do? He hears and gives justice.

My friend Jeff reminds me of the widow. Jeff prays like he means it. When I worked in Portland, it wasn't uncommon for him to fast and dedicate long periods of time in prayer. He even sought mentors to grow in his relationship with God.

One night, I went to a restaurant with Jeff and four other friends. Pancakes bathed in maple syrup were steaming on our plates. The conversation was just as delicious. The jokes were spontaneous and the comments sincere. At the end of the night, we prayed for one another.

My request to God was for a job. I'd graduated college but had only found part-time work. It's hard to pay off student loans on that money. Thankfully, it fell on Jeff to pray for me.

The very next day, I got a phone call from Food 4 Less, a grocery store one block from my house. They interviewed me, and soon I was clocking in.

What a speedy turnaround! No wonder Jesus said, "Will he delay long over them? I tell you, he will give justice to them speedily."

He wants us to pray without losing heart. Well, when it comes to encouragement, few things bring you back to life like an answered prayer—especially if you get a paycheck along with it.

I asked God for a job, but He gave me much more. There in Food 4 Less, I enjoyed the physical nature of the work: pushing carts, walking, lifting boxes. I liked to see the before-and-after of my cleaning.

After working hard, the apex of my night was the walk home through the parking lot. At eleven o'clock, Portland was already sleeping. You could hear cars passing by on the boulevard every once in a while, like the nocturnal breathing of the city.

I met interesting people at Food 4 Less. Dan was the employee who trained me. He was nineteen and had graduated from the high school near my house. He sported a tattoo that read, *Dream like you'll live forever. Live like you'll die tomorrow.* His dream was to play guitar in an acoustic band, but I sure hoped he wouldn't die tomorrow.

One winter evening at work, I saw a young couple. They walked through the produce section holding hands. There by the avocados, they stopped and looked deeply into each other's eyes. They put their hands on the other's face. They smiled. This was the unbridled delight of being together that one rarely sees except in the eyes of an infant.

The most interesting person I met at Food 4 Less was Charles. He made the most of our city's recycling system. Machines at grocery stores would pay cash depending on how many containers someone recycled. That money was vital for Charles because he lived on the street, homeless.

On one occasion, it was nine at night. Charles stood in front of the machines with his shopping cart full of cans in grimy plastic bags. The ragged coat he wore was almost in worse condition than those plastic bags. While he was putting the cans in the machine one by one, he blurted things out, speaking over his right shoulder: "No! God isn't like that!" and "Satan doesn't have her. Stop!" It looked like he was arguing with someone, but he couldn't have been. No one else was there.

I was servicing one of the machines, so I asked him, "Is everything working well for you tonight?"

"Yep."

"Well, if you need anything at all, push that button, and I'll come out to help you."

Before I could go, he asked me a question: "Hey, you're a Christian, right?"

Surprised that he would say that—we were strangers, after all—I responded tentatively, "Yeah. Yes, I am."

"Well," he continued, "the devil has been tormenting me for a while now."

I asked him what was happening. His explanation didn't clarify much for me, but I knew for sure that he was afflicted. He had gone to various people, even a Catholic priest, looking for help. Nothing seemed to ease his pain.

"So, what do I do?" he asked me.

What do you think Charles should have done? There beside the machine, I thought for a moment. *What would the widow in the parable do for him? What would Jeff do? They would intercede with all their might for this man. They would fight for his soul on their knees.* With this in mind, I knew what to do.

"Charles, Jesus said one time that some demons don't leave us except through prayer and fasting. Could I fast and pray for you?"

He nodded.

The next week, I saw Charles again. There we were, as always, in front of the recycling machines. I asked him how he was.

"Whatever it was that you did, it worked!"

Glory to God. Walking home in the cool air, I couldn't help but sing to Him. He was teaching me to pray without losing heart because He does respond.

Food 4 Less was my night job. I spent my mornings in a whole different environment. I was a Spanish teacher in my first months as an educator. That alone felt scary enough, but education wasn't even the major I studied! The key word for circumstances like this is "survival." Therefore, I went to Brad, my old high school teacher. I needed help urgently.

If my class could be a shadow of what Brad's had been, it would be a big success. Brad gave us Spanish names only for his class. One time, he took us to a Mexican restaurant so we could order in Spanish. His class had what they can't print in textbooks: love for your neighbor. That was because Brad dedicated himself to pray outside of school. His love for people made him intercede for them.

Brad told me that when he was young in the faith, he saw blind people on a daily basis. For two years, he noticed at least one blind person on the way to work or out and about in the city.

What started off as a strange observation turned into a burden. But what could he do for them? The only cure for blindness that Brad knew was Jesus. So he went up to the blind people and on various occasions, he cried out to God to heal them.

UP UNTIL THIS POINT, WE'VE SEEN THAT GOD ANSWERS US. HE participates in our lives. It's incredible! So, why did Jesus have to teach us to "pray and not lose heart"?

Because sometimes what we're about to see happen to Brad will also happen to us. Brad prayed for those blind people, but after saying "amen," nothing happened. The heavens didn't open up, and beams of light did not descend.

There was only silence.

Before continuing with Brad's story, we have to go to a crucial moment in the Bible to understand God's silence. We have to go to Gethsemane.

Jesus was in the olive orchard where He regularly went to be alone and pray. This night would be His last because in just a few hours they'd capture Him and kill Him. And Jesus knew it.

And they went to a place called Gethsemane. And he said to his disciples, "Sit here while I pray." And he took with him

Peter and James and John, and began to be greatly distressed and troubled. And he said to them, "My soul is very sorrowful, even to death. Remain here and watch." And going a little farther, he fell on the ground and prayed that, if it were possible, the hour might pass from him. And he said, "Abba, Father, all things are possible for you. Remove this cup from me. Yet not what I will, but what you will." … And again he went away and prayed, saying the same words. (Mark 14:32–36, 39)

Here was Jesus pouring out the sorrow of His soul in the form of prayer. He wasn't reciting words; He was crying out. And He did it to such an extent that sweat fell from His forehead like drops of blood.

And what was God's reply?

Silence.

The "cup" wasn't removed. Jesus had to drink it to the dregs. That same night, soldiers took Him captive. They tortured Him, following the brutal practices of the Romans. Naked on the cross, His suffering was publicly exposed. In the uproar of that night, His best friends abandoned Him. Then, from the cross, Jesus cried out to the Father one more time: "My God, my God, why have you forsaken me?" (Mark 15:34).

When I depend on a response from God and don't hear anything, that silence leaves me dazed and confused. I would prefer to be stunned by a bomb blast because at least in that case I would know what was happening. But silence is something else. *Could it be that I don't have enough faith? Could it be I've just been shouting to the void?*

The followers of Jesus must have thought the same thing when His body was taken down from the cross. As they lay down to sleep that night, their leader was lying in the grave. I don't know if they slept or if God's silence gave them insomnia.

Perhaps they tried to understand it. Jesus had made an impossible request. He had asked to not suffer the agony of the cross, but Jesus's entire life had been leading Him to that moment. That's why He came. How could God rescue Him and at the same time sacrifice Him?

As far as the disciples could see that night, the answer to Jesus's prayer was "no."

Some of your prayers are impossible too. You prayed for something, but the years of your life were not enough to see it fulfilled. The spread of the cancerous cells couldn't be stopped. The hurricane couldn't be held back. The will in the innermost part of that person couldn't be bent toward you.

As far as you can see now, the answer to your prayer is "no."

Nevertheless:

> In the days of his flesh, Jesus offered up prayers and supplications, with loud cries and tears, to him who was able to save him from death, and he was heard because of his reverence. (Hebrews 5:7)

Jesus *was* heard because in eternity God can say "yes" to impossible requests.

Generally, we think of death as the conclusion, but on the other side of it is eternity. We measure this mortal life in decades, but centuries and millennia are insignificant measures for endless life. God resurrected His Son, and Jesus eternally enjoys the comfort and joy and belonging He feared losing at the cross.

In eternity, God gives you what you ultimately ask for. He sees through the fog of your circumstances to the heart of what you request. In my case, I have asked and still ask God for a wife. The heart of my request is intimacy, belonging, suitable help, beauty that takes my breath away.

I've spent over a decade pursuing marriage, and I'm well

acquainted with the word "no." With each passing year and each unsuccessful attempt, it feels like the answer to my prayer is a stone-cold "no." But regarding what I am ultimately looking for, I know His answer is "yes."

Maybe you object as I sometimes do: If God responds to us in eternity, what about that word "speedily"? Isn't He supposed to respond without delay?

However, "delay" doesn't indicate a measurable time but instead a relative descriptor. If I wait three hours to connect with my friend over the telephone, it feels like a delay. But if in those same three hours, he traveled to Mexico from North Carolina, then I would marvel at how fast the trip was. Three weeks can feel like a delay if you're waiting for a reply to a text message. Three days can feel like a delay if you're waiting to eat. Three seconds can feel like a delay if your hand is in a fire.

If God gives me what I yearn for on this side of death or the other, what is the difference? It will be mine for eternity without end.

LET'S RETURN TO BRAD AND HIS PRAYERS. A FEW YEARS AGO, God led Brad to preach on the streets. At that time, he didn't know what street preaching was about. He had never seen anyone do it. Nonetheless, he gathered his courage, tied his shoes, and stood out on the sidewalk. Hundreds of people passed by him, faces looking forward. Brad was a stone in the middle of a river of people flowing around him. Minutes passed by. He dried his sweaty hands on his pants. His foot involuntarily tapped on the concrete. *Okay, here we go!* He took a step and... ran to the bathroom.

A few minutes later, he was back on the sidewalk. He squeezed his eyes shut. He cleared his throat. He began to preach.

Brad didn't return home wondering what effect he'd had,

because he saw a person put their faith in Christ that day. It was the start of his weekly custom of street preaching. He went to Pioneer Courthouse Square in Portland, Oregon, to tell people what God had done for him. For ten years, Brad saw at least one person decide to trust Christ every time he went.

"WHEN THE SON OF MAN COMES, WILL HE FIND FAITH ON earth?" asked Jesus. I think He will because Brad and Jeff are here. I hope He finds faith in you and me as well. I want persistence that doesn't lose heart, that sees when God does justice to His chosen ones. I want to pray like I mean it.

EIGHT

WITH YOU

DON'T GO IT ALONE

In the first chapter, I told you I went on an excursion through caves. Let's go back to that trip.

The day after my leap into the darkness, I was back in the city of Monterrey. I had on my best tie and newly polished shoes. I walked close to buildings because I didn't want to sweat and stain my shirt and résumé. The heat was unreal. I'm pretty sure air-conditioning in northern Mexico is a basic human right. Through the spaces between the buildings, I could see towering rock walls in the near distance; these were the mountains that surround Monterrey, the city that would be my new home.

Did I say "my new home"? That's right. I had worked for four years as a Spanish teacher in Oregon, and I had paid off my student loans. My next adventure was calling me. I planned on moving to Mexico that summer, and I didn't want to arrive without a job—thus the reason for my midday stroll, the destination being a local institute.

I breathed in slowly to control my nerves. I feared coming face to face with an uninterested administrator who would ask me dryly, "Who are you?" All the emails I had sent to these prospective schools must have gone to the moon because no one had replied to me.

I crossed a street, and from the other side, I could see the sign I had been looking for: *International House*. It looked just like it had on Google. Honestly, my job-hunting strategy was to search for "English school," walk to every pin that showed up on Maps, and ask for a job. I passed through the gate to International House and went to the reception area. With the most confidence I could muster, I asked to speak with the director. Don't let my cool-headed demeanor fool you. I felt like a kid trespassing on private property. Waiting for the director to come out, I tried to remember the interview tips I had heard: *"Dress for success." Okay, check. "Arrive on time." Well, in this case, I don't have an appointment. I'll give it a check anyway. "Relax." Che—*

"Good afternoon." The greeting brought me back to the moment. Before me stood a man in a suit and tie with his hand extended. He was the director. I shook his hand as he continued, "Welcome to International House. How can I help you?"

I smiled, looked him in the eye, and said, "My name is Andrew Moses. I'm a teacher, and I'm here to apply for work."

An hour later, I walked out the front door with a smile from ear to ear. Outside, an American guy awaited me. In his shorts and sleeveless shirt, he was a tad more comfortable in the heat.

"Alex," I said, "you're not going to believe it!"

I didn't tell you, did I? I'd come to Monterrey in good company. Alex has been my close friend since junior high. In high school, we drove a van across the United States together. We snowboarded the powder of Mount Hood together. We went off to college in Ohio together. We moved back to Portland and rented an apartment together.

Now here we were on another adventure. We got on a city

bus. Seated aboard it, I told Alex how the interview had gone. He listened and nodded every once in a while. He wore a hat turned backward that made his ears stick out a little. "They haven't offered me a job yet," I continued, "but they want to schedule another appointment."

Alex in turn told me about the mountain he'd hiked to see the Asta Bandera, a huge Mexican flag. He'd done that while I was at International House. Hiking and extreme sports had always been his thing. I leaned back in the bus seat and crossed one leg over the other. I closed my eyes for a second to savor the experience. Here I was, in an unfamiliar city on streets with names I had never heard of, one month away from being unemployed, but I knew one thing for certain: Alex was with me.

The single fact that Alex was with me changed everything. When we have people that love us, we can face anything. That's why this verse means so much to me:

> Be strong and courageous. Do not fear or be in dread of them, for it is the Lord your God who goes with you. He will not leave you or forsake you. (Deuteronomy 31:6)

God goes with us. In the Garden of Eden, God walked with Adam and Eve. In the wilderness, God guided Moses and the Israelites to their new home. In the days of the kings of Israel, God spoke with prophets. God was with us in flesh and blood when Jesus came to live among us. Today God lives in us through the Consoler, the Holy Spirit.

That's a lot of people God has walked with! In fact, God is "the trustworthy God, maintaining his covenant and his *loyal love* with those who love him and with those who keep his commandments to a thousand generations" (Deuteronomy 7:9 LEB). *A thousand generations!*

When the verse says "loyal love," that is an English translation of the Hebrew word *hesed*. It's the kind of love that's constant, steadfast, always-and-forever. We mean so much to God that *hesed* appears 250 times in the Bible. His love didn't run out on us then, and it's still loyal today.

My friend and I made a good team in Monterrey. I was Frodo with the mission of finding a job, and Alex was the wizard Gandalf with a smartphone as his staff (in those days, I had a flip phone). He amazed me with the spells he cast: he touched the screen, and a taxi showed up. He did it again, and —*boom!*—we had an Airbnb penthouse. At night, his GPS directed us to Tacos Primo, the most delicious place for tacos downtown. As for me, being the Spanish speaker of the duo, it was my job to translate when we arrived at the places Alex guided us to.

For five days, we walked together from one English institute to another. After each one, I processed with my friend: What did I like about the school? What were my reservations? All the ground we walked was unknown, but little by little, I was finding my way.

Obviously, the trip was beneficial for me, but years later, I asked Alex why he had traveled with me. We had gone to Monterrey, not Cancun. Instead of swimming at the beach, we walked through the smog of factories. We had fun, but I don't think Alex ever would have said by himself, "I want to travel to another country and visit an industrial metropolis." And I doubt it would have been his first choice to go on a trip that would leave him stumbling over his rudimentary Spanish.

This trip cost Alex since they don't give out taxis, tacos, and Airbnb accommodations for free. Because Alex was a financial analyst, he knew about investment. He was a careful spender. That's the reason I asked him why he'd gone with me.

Alex responded, "You were at a crossroads in your life, and I didn't want you to go it alone."

THESE WORDS SEEMED POETIC TO ME. I WANTED TO FRAME them and hang them on the wall because that's how friendships should be. I know they should be this way because Christ said so:

> This is my commandment, that you love one another as I have loved you. Greater love has no one than this, that someone lay down his life for his friends. (John 15:12–13)

Jesus wants you to love like He loved—a love that leads you to give. Jesus gave importance to people; their needs moved Him. He gave His ears and eyes and undivided attention. His relationship with His disciples was warm, so He gave them nicknames. The disciples weren't good listeners and got into trouble because of it, so Jesus gave them patience. But that's not all. He pulled them out of that trouble by giving them what they needed: the truth.

When you love, you give. My Mexican friends generously give their time. My American friends freely give their money. In fact, the last five years of my salary at NOE International has been paid because my friends have donated to the cause each month.

But sometimes you give and you feel like it kills you. It's not comfortable. What you are giving is not extra or left over; if you give it, it'll disrupt your plans. Many people see a clear dividing line here. They see the edge of a cliff and won't go any further.

Jesus did.

When He gave Himself to be crucified, He was saying there wasn't anything He wouldn't give in order to save us.

This is true loyalty; this is *hesed*. Jesus tells us to love each other the same way.

Years after walking among the skyscrapers of Monterrey, Alex and I met up again in Mexico. We got off a bus that ran between nearby towns. We stood on the shoulder of a highway that traversed the back of a mountain. From there, we could see the Pacific Ocean and its vast blue horizon. A flotilla of clouds drifted over the waters.

Weeks earlier, Alex had called me. He needed to clear his head from the stress of his routine. What better way than by being in communion with God in nature? He invited me to join him on his bro-venture. With this plan, we went to the coast of Jalisco for a few days on the beach.

First, we needed a place to stay. Alex found one on the internet, but we'd have to hike to it. With our huge outdoor packs on, Alex led the way. We crossed the highway to the jungle on the other side. It was alive with insects and birds. We could hear an almost electric buzz from it all. Among the broad leaves of the underbrush, we found a dirt road. We had seen a map on the phone and knew this road should lead to our destination.

We followed the path into the jungle. We went up hills and down them, Alex and I nothing but ants on the spine of the mountain. After several miles, the forest opened up, and a meadow spread out before us. The sun beat down on us. I wondered how the wildflowers had survived it. I started to get thirsty.

We made our pilgrimage on a forgotten dusty road. Far from civilization, no one had paved it, and as far as we could see, no one was traveling it. If it weren't for the mooing of cows in the distance, I would have said we were completely alone.

We took off our shirts to tie them on our heads like Arabs.

To lift my spirits, Alex told me about the pictures he'd seen of the Airbnb. It was a complex of tropical cabanas. Soon we'd be lying in hammocks in a paradise of landscaped gardens. Air-conditioning and ice-cold drinks were awaiting us.

Where the meadow gave way again to the jungle, barbwire blocked our path. It stretched between two posts on either side of the road. "Do we jump it?" I wondered aloud. Here in the wilderness, the GPS didn't work to orient us. Alex had to lead us by memory. We jumped it.

For another forty minutes, we followed the road. It got muddy under our feet in the forest hollow. By this time, my legs were shaking with fatigue.

Suddenly, a silhouette appeared in the trees, straight lines among the natural curves: a building. We sped up our pace to see cabanas in the forest.

We let out a laugh of triumph because we had made it! The owner of the place gave us a warm welcome. We took off our backpacks and spotted a crystalline river that flowed beside the resort. At the river's edge, they had built a terrace with a fireplace and comfortable lawn furniture. There, we relaxed with those ice-cold drinks while the twilight deepened the reds of the sky into shades of purple.

ONE DAY, YOU'LL ARRIVE HOME, THE ONE GOD IS PREPARING for you. Your Father will give you a welcome like you've never experienced. Meanwhile, stay the course. You will have moments when you feel more lost and thirsty than Alex and I did on that dirt road. You will have moments when you don't see anyone around, and you'll wonder where God is. But He is there. Know His words and let His voice guide you. The Holy Spirit will go with you.

Then you, as one never truly abandoned by God, can be a source of *hesed* in the lives of your friends like Alex is for me.

Together, we will arrive, because His love is loyal.

NINE

YOUR INNER WORLD

WHAT TO DO BEFORE POINTING THE FINGER

There is a whole world out there. There are social movements, there is economic slowdown, there are geopolitical power plays, there are hurricanes and earthquakes, there is globalization and industries that benefit from it, there are civil wars and world wars, there are dictatorships that don't end, laws that don't get enforced, and deserts that don't produce.

And there, in the middle of it all, are you.

Those who try to change the world discover it isn't so easy. It usually works the other way: the world changes you. Some people go so far as to say that who you are is formed under the pressure of outside forces, that you are nothing but the product of your environment.

But one Jewish survivor of the Nazi Holocaust didn't agree. He wrote the following:

> ... the sort of person the prisoner became was the result of an inner decision, and not the result of camp influences alone. Fundamentally, therefore, any man can, even under such circumstances, decide what shall become of him—mentally and spiritually. He may retain his human dignity even in a concentration camp.[1]

Out there is a stormy world, but with this quote from his book *Man's Search for Meaning*, Viktor Frankl reminds us there is also a heart here inside. Frankl, a psychologist and author, focused his work on the interior of his patients. They couldn't change their past or revive their loved ones, but they could put order into their life starting today.

I'd like to tell you two stories about what happed inside of me while I lived in Monterrey.

AFTER ALEX AND I HAD SCOPED OUT THE CITY IN THE SPRING, I made the move that summer. Stepping off the plane, pure adrenaline pumped through my veins. It was one of the few times when I didn't have keys or a cell phone in my pants pockets. That's because I actually didn't have either of those things. I didn't have any friends or family or anyone to stay with. It was a fresh start. The only concrete thing I had walking out of the airport was my job, and I went to work the following day.

I left my Airbnb early to report for duty at the institute. To my surprise, I wasn't giving English lessons in a classroom but rather in conference rooms at different businesses around the city. I was training their employees.

I had to learn the bus routes. On board, I couldn't take my eyes off my new city: surreal murals in shouty colors, skyscrapers dressed in blue shining glass, even an industrial precinct in decay that would have been the perfect place to film *The Walking Dead*. Between classes, I found myself bursting with hope. Each café I discovered was my new favorite, and inside were people who could be my new friends.

I told all this to my family and friends in Portland. I had a laptop and Wi-Fi in my Airbnb, and we kept in contact through these means. I didn't feel so alone when they were a video call away (Thanks, Facebook!).

But after a few weeks of living in Monterrey, the excitement turned into stress. I needed a place to live. I had only three days left in the Airbnb. Like a good millennial, I turned to technology. I opened my laptop but noticed the Wi-Fi wasn't working in my room. I knocked on the door downstairs to talk to the owner before remembering she had gone away on vacation.

No problem—I had a few pesos and could go to a café to use their Wi-Fi. With my backpack almost packed, I searched for my laptop charger. My battery had just a sliver of power left. I checked all the outlets and under the bed. I couldn't find it. I began searching systematically, opening the closet and every drawer. I looked over every surface and in every nook. *Where's the $*&%ing cable?*

With no digital means of looking for an apartment, I began riding my bike around neighborhoods searching the facades of the houses for a sign that read *Rooms for Rent*. I bought newspapers, looked for apartments in their classified ads, and made phone calls. Every clue I followed led to another dead end.

Meanwhile, I had to teach my English classes without my digital library of resources. On top of that, an annoyance on par with a cloud of mosquitos, I couldn't communicate with anyone without Wi-Fi. *¡¡&%$·*@!!*

On a Monday morning after my first class, I'd gone back to the apartment I would imminently be leaving. Sick and tired of all my recent troubles, I blew up. The people on the other sides of each of the four walls of my room heard every swear word in the English *AND* Spanish languages. I yelled into a pillow. I stomped back and forth. I grunted. I exploded all my frustrations until I lay exhausted on my bed.

It's tempting to think my words disappeared as soon as the sound of my voice did. But I remembered Jesus said it didn't work like that:

For out of the abundance of the heart the mouth speaks.
The good person out of his good treasure brings forth good,
and the evil person out of his evil treasure brings forth evil.
I tell you, on the day of judgment people will give account
for every careless word they speak, for by your words you
will be justified, and by your words you will be condemned.
(Matthew 12:34–37)

This gave me pause. *Am I an angry person?* I didn't like what
was coming out of me. I reflected on the words I had been
letting loose, both in that moment and recently, especially the
biting criticism I harbored against people. I would have to give
an account for these sentiments one day. That made a shiver
run down my spine.

I sat down to resolve my attitude, and I always do this best
with a pencil in my hand. In my diary appears this scribble:

I choose to recognize the goodness and generosity of God in
this moment of stress.

I choose to put a stop to the curses and anger. I will
exhaust all my options, I will try everything I can, and then
I will leave the rest in God's hands. I'll give Him margin to
provide.

I am bigger than this setback. God is bigger than this
setback.

Today I am so grateful for that tight spot because it made
me put my inner world in order. In the end, that is what lasts.
Let the exterior circumstances change as they may.

With one day left before I'd become homeless, I walked
down a street I normally didn't take and saw a sign that adver-
tised a room for rent. In five minutes, I was in the apartment
looking at it. In four hours, I was signing a contract, making it
my new home.

.   .   .

AFTER THIS MOVE, ANOTHER OPPORTUNITY CAME ALONG FOR me to order my inner world. It was in a teacher training course. When International House hired me, they stipulated in the contract that I take a Cambridge University course. It would be a year of research, teaching observation, and writing. It would also be a year of five-hour classes every Friday.

In the last few minutes of one class, already dying to go, I leaned over to my classmate Lalo. I whispered to him that we should go for tacos. He liked the idea. When class got out, we made a plan. He and our professor, Orlando, would go in Lalo's car while I went on my bike. It was no big deal, as they'd get there a little earlier and order for me. I'd pay them back when I arrived. I took advantage of his car's trunk and asked him to take my backpack. It must've weighed at least forty pounds with my books and the groceries I had bought earlier in the afternoon. I figured I'd just pick it up after dinner.

I arrived at Tacos Primo. It was packed with people. The line looked like an audience at a concert and went out the door. And for good reason too: those tacos were mad tasty. I pushed my way through the door and looked for my friend. It would be easy to spot him; if anyone rose head and shoulders above everyone else like a Latino version of the Hulk, it was Lalo.

But I couldn't find him. I walked around the restaurant. *Nope. Okay, one more pass just to be sure. Nada. Well, maybe they got confused and went to the tacos place around the corner.* I checked; they weren't there either. No problem, I'd just call him. As I felt my pants pockets, my stomach dropped. My cell phone was in my backpack ... in his trunk.

Defeated, I got on my bike and started for home when something else came to mind. *Oh, perfect!* The books I needed for my presentation the next morning were in my backpack too. Upset, I yelled to the night sky of Monterrey, "Why can't I trust anyone on the face of the freakin' planet?"

Just when my indignation was gaining speed, the words of Jesus came and made me hit the brakes:

> Judge not, that you be not judged. For with the judgment you pronounce you will be judged, and with the measure you use it will be measured to you. Why do you see the speck that is in your brother's eye, but do not notice the log that is in your own eye? Or how can you say to your brother, "Let me take the speck out of your eye," when there is the log in your own eye? You hypocrite, first take the log out of your own eye, and then you will see clearly to take the speck out of your brother's eye. (Mathew 7:1–5)

It felt natural to point a finger at Lalo. He aroused the activist in me that wants to change the world—the world that Lalo was a part of. But this night, I decided to hear Jesus out. I arrived at my house and rested my bike against the wall. Then I sat on my bed and in prayer checked my eyes for logs.

I have always been the kind of person who has just a few tight friends. I've been accused more than once of having a "bromance." The bad thing about that is I've uprooted a lot of people from my life that I didn't think measured up to my standard of a friend. I know, it's ugly. I've tried to reestablish contact with a few of the people I distanced, but it was too late. To them, I was just a judgmental guy.

This night, would I let Lalo's slip-up end our budding friendship?

I decided to give Lalo the benefit of the doubt.

The rest of the story went like this: Lalo and Orlando got to the taco place and saw the crowd of people. Since they were eager to eat, they decided to go to a less busy place. Lalo sent me a message with the new location. While they were at the other place, he saw that I hadn't responded, so he called me. Then it hit him: he heard my cell phone ringing in the trunk. They went back to Tacos Primo.

"Hey, have you seen a white guy around here recently?" Lalo asked a worker.

"Yeah, but he left."

Now that he had all my stuff, Lalo worried that he might also have my house keys. He knew I lived close to a park called La Alameda, so they drove around the park, windows rolled down, yelling, "Andrewwwwww! Andrewwwwww!"

They were afraid I was going to spend the night homeless. The next day in class, we had a good laugh about the whole thing.

Jesus taught me that when I stop searching for faults in others, it is much easier to make friends. And you get to belly laugh with your friends.

IF YOU ARE STRUGGLING TO ORDER YOUR INNER WORLD, YOU know it's an endless war. You march in with your New Year's resolutions, but wave after wave of distractions try to defeat you. There in the battlefield lie wounded all the virtues you had hoped would triumph.

Don't give up. The same Jesus who told you not to judge doesn't disapprove of you: "For God did not send his Son into the world to condemn the world, but in order that the world might be saved through him" (John 3:17).

His focus is on saving you. And that's great because you need salvation, maybe from the circumstances out there, but absolutely from within. If "out of the abundance of the heart the mouth speaks," I see that my heart is the problem. My heart is bent on sinning: if I don't fall in lust, I fall in self-pity; if I don't fall in self-pity, I fall in arrogance. I'm bent on sinning.

Nevertheless, Jesus Christ saves us with the surgery only He is capable of providing: "And I will give you a new heart, and a new spirit I will put within you. And I will remove the

heart of stone from your flesh and give you a heart of flesh"
(Ezekiel 36:26).

HISTORY IS ADVANCING TOWARD A GRAND FINALE IN WHICH THE
whole earth will be transformed. It won't come through
protests or awareness-raising or legislation. It will come
through God, who makes all things new, even the human
heart. So, friend, don't give up. With hope for that day, take
care of your inner world.

TEN

COPY AND PASTE

HOW TO TREAT OTHERS

A couple of years ago, I bought a new laptop. Opening the lid and clicking through the empty folders felt like walking into a house without furniture. Maybe I'm a nerd, but I missed my programs and files. So I took out my old hard drive and plugged it into my new laptop. On that drive was the digital representation of my whole life: photos of my family, thoughts written in my diary from years ago, lyrics to my original songs, and thousands of MP3s that I had bought. In three minutes, it was all transferred to my laptop.

That is magic: copy and paste. You don't need to know Java or HTML; just copy and paste. Jesus gives you an equally impressive teaching: "As you wish that others would do to you, do so to them" (Luke 6:31).

It's that simple. Jesus invites you to think about what you wish for. If you could work on a team in the most gratifying way, what would each member do? When you walk into a classroom, how do you want your classmates to receive you? How do you want your family to talk to you? Once you imagine it—*copy*!

What comes next is also straightforward but requires effort. *Paste*. Everything you just imagined others doing for you

—you do for them. Stick it to them. Apply love like a kid in kindergarten applies glue to her arts and crafts.

MANY PEOPLE DON'T REALIZE WHAT JESUS ACTUALLY SAID. Maybe they didn't read attentively, but if you ask them, they recite the verse backward: "Don't do to others what you wish they wouldn't do to you." Perhaps they think Jesus said that because it makes some sense. They don't want anyone to steal their car, so they don't steal cars. They'd prefer to not have their house burned down, so they don't throw Molotov cocktails. They can live their whole lives like this, more or less shielded from attacks, more or less innocent of attacking.

But they miss something. Personal relationships don't grow out of the inaction of "don't do." How do you passively fall in love? Passively forge an alliance? Make friendships? Look, it's possible to be negligent, even a narcissist and still fulfill the motto, "Don't do to others what you wish they wouldn't do to you."

Jesus said "do" because He wants us to take the initiative.

THESE DAYS, THE GYM HAS HELPED ME UNDERSTAND MORE about what Jesus said. I started to lift weights for the first time in years, and oh how I have gotten thirsty. One time, I drank a liter and a half of water. When the pangs of thirst overcome you, when you can't even swallow your spit, you can't enjoy anything, not even your favorite movie. I guess that's why the theater can charge you an arm and a leg for a soda.

It's hard to believe it when it burns, but thirst exists for your good. Like the majority of physical pain, it's the body's way of saying, "There is a problem. Fix it." The thirst of your spirit helps you identify what "you wish that others would do to you."

Jesus doesn't want you to die in the desert. "Do so to

them" becomes a spring that satisfies those around you and you as well. If it hurts when others ignore you, answer your messages. If you desire recognition, thank others. If you want company, make the invite—then just see if they don't return the love.

SOME PEOPLE DON'T DESERVE "COPY AND PASTE." LET ME TELL you about one I met recently.

It happened during the hot days of summer. The plants were withering in the flowerpots on our rooftop. But in the house next door, the lawn was deep green. Their plants were enjoying an oasis. Through the window, I could hear our little neighbor splashing in a kiddie pool. And the hose that transported the water that made these things possible was attached... to our spigot. Our neighbor was stealing our water! The bill that month was jaw-dropping.

With people like this, I don't feel like copying or pasting or giving them anything—well, maybe a whack upside the head. I opted for something more subtle: I took the hose inside our house. I thought we would surely hear a *knock-knock* on the door, and we would see a blushing lady, and she would apologize. I would then return the hose and ask her to use her own water in the future. But nobody knocked on our door. I went out the next day, and what did I see? Another hose connected to our spigot! So I took it off and put it in the back with the other one. In case that didn't make my point sufficiently clear, I took out a screwdriver and took apart the spigot so it physically wouldn't be possible for our neighbors to steal from us anymore. *Okay,* I thought, *now she is going to have to come and chat with us.*

That night, I got home after work. I parked my car, and while the windows were rolling up, I heard the sound of flowing water. I opened the door of my Honda, and there at my feet was ANOTHER hose attached to our now repaired spigot. At that point, if I had been water, I would have been boiling and bound to scald anyone near me.

It turned out that the woman had come to our house, and our Chinese friend that lived with us had opened the door. I don't know what Asian norms dictate when there is an interpersonal conflict, but he returned the hose and apologized to her. *He* apologized to *her?* Seriously? That was not the moral of the story, and as far as I was concerned, it wouldn't be the end of it either.

I knocked on the neighbor's door, and the woman opened up. She was wearing a suit, business casual, with simple black earrings. I think she was an administrator at a school. The bags under her eyes and the apathy in them gave the impression her patience had run out many hours ago. If she were the principal of that school, she would have been the type that made kids cry.

"What do you want?" Grammatically, it was a question, but by the rough tone of her voice, it seemed more like a dare. I breathed slowly and began to lay out my complaint. She cut me off and rolled out her perspective. Then she said she didn't have to talk to me because my housemate Grant was the principal renter.

At this point, it would be useful to mention that our neighbor was the owner of our house. As such, she felt she had the right to take our water. And because of this hose debacle, she informed me she wasn't going to help us in the future. If the house needed maintenance, too bad.

I hadn't been expecting that. And if that encounter had left me disoriented, I read something in the Bible the following morning and felt even more perplexed. I broke away from Luke 6:31 and saw the title of the section where that verse is found. I didn't like what I saw. I felt challenged. It read, *Love Your Enemies.*

When it comes to enemies, it's easy to sink into the mire of victim mentality. "I was the victim first," affirms one. "But you hurt me badly, and I'm *more* of a victim," objects the other. After the counterattack and the counter-counterattack, where does it end? The more we struggle in this mud, justifying ourselves and adding up offenses, the more we get stuck.

I think the woman next door had reason to take offense at me, mainly because of my first encounter with her twenty-something-year-old son. He wanted me to translate into English a master's-level thesis he had pirated off the Internet. Given that I had dedicated my adult life to the proper use of language, I wasn't going to be his accomplice in this rip-off. It was garbage, and I let him know it. The next day, I apologized for the severity of my words, but first impressions are hard to erase. My neighbors already saw themselves as martyrs.

Now, with the water incident, was I going to feel the same?

I don't want to spend my days rolling around in the mud; I believe we were born for the mountaintop view. This is the higher perspective: understanding that you and I are not the injured party.

> For one will scarcely die for a righteous person—though perhaps for a good person one would dare even to die—but God shows his love for us in that while we were still sinners, Christ died for us. (Romans 5:7–8)

We are all the next-door neighbor. We steal God's glory from Him. His blessings flow like water, but we don't appreciate Him or what He gives. And even while we were sinners, Jesus took the initiative: He loved us; He loved His enemies.

How could I, who received so great a love as this, refuse love to my enemy?

With this in mind, I rang my neighbor's doorbell. I had practiced the conversation: I was going to take responsibility for my part in our skirmishes, specifically for having acted rashly without speaking to her first. I also decided not to mention her part in the issue; my purpose was not to win an argument but to win a neighbor. Therefore, I also brought a show of goodwill—a tub of ice cream.

She opened the door, and from that point on, the encounter did not go as planned. She didn't want to hear any words of reconciliation. Although I didn't blame her at all, she gave me a defensive monologue about how she wasn't a bad person. And, arms crossed, she made it clear she didn't want ice cream. I left it on the welcome mat of her house in case she changed her mind.

My friend Joel had once said to me, "You shouldn't ask, 'Why is this happening to me?' You should ask, 'For what purpose is this happening to me?'" Now that I reflect on it, if it wasn't for the friction with my neighbor, I never would have paid attention to her. Frankly, when I come home after work, I do so intending to relax. If it weren't for this run-in, I also wouldn't have thought, *How do I wish to be treated so that I can treat my neighbor that way?*

For starters, I like to be greeted, so I greeted her. I like gifts, so I gave her a traditional cake at Christmas. One time, I left an orchid on her front lawn. I liked it and thought she might like it too. It's not a lot, I know, but I tried to keep my eyes open for opportunities.

One day, an opportunity peeked through the open door of our house. With all the innocence of his six years, our little neighbor asked, "Hey, whatcha doin'?" We were having a party, and he must have heard the cumbia music. He came in and participated in the games. We gave him steak tacos. At another party, he ate ice cream with us. They say if you want to show love to a parent, treat their kid well.

God allows enemies into our lives, and like Joel, I believe He has a purpose in doing so; His purpose is, simply, that our enemies be loved.

In my apartment in Monterrey, there was one bed, one refrigerator, one stove, one bicycle, and only one occupant: me. When I got home at night, I would climb up to the rooftop to contemplate the metropolis. I would let my feet hang over the edge and allow the warm breeze to wash over my face. I could hear the soft music from the patio of some nearby house. Amber-colored lights filtered out the windows around me. Some windows were open, and I could hear when the people burst into laughter. Oh, how I wanted to share the serenity of that view. But among four million people, I didn't have anyone.

This thirst of my spirit was telling me: "There's a problem; fix it."

The church I attended was huge; thousands of people came and went every Sunday. If I were a Christian spy, it would have been the ideal place to go—anyone can be anonymous in a big church. But I didn't want espionage. How was I going to make friends in that environment?

I remembered what Jesus said and thought: *It's on me to initiate with them. I'm going to be the friend I wish I had.* And I did it with the help of Mexico's most beloved food: tacos. If someone seemed alone and out of place, I invited them to tacos after the service. If someone seemed nice? Tacos. A friend of an acquaintance? Tacos. And if a group was already going for tacos, I'd just invite myself. As you already saw with my neighbor, I'm not too good at first impressions; I usually need two or three. The good thing about sharing a meal is that you can chat for a while, scratch more than the surface of the other. I left those meals feeling less alone.

As weeks went by, the acquaintances from the taco outings became my friends from flag football. And my friends from flag football also played cards. I invited and invited, and soon we were exploring mountains and drinking good coffee together.

One Sunday afternoon, I went to an open mic at Cronopios, a bohemian café frequented by poets and singer-song-writers. That night, I was going to play some original songs. I got there early to save seats for a couple of my new friends.

I sat at a small table with my tea. I tried to control my stage fright by looking at the modern art paintings on the wall. At this time, my friend Diego came in. With a huge smile and two hands in the air, he greeted me with a shout. Behind him came eight other people! I was dumbfounded. I couldn't believe so many people wanted to see me play the guitar.

With five on the couch and three on the carpet, they laughed and cheered me on when I sang—and they became my close friends from Monterrey.

Our friendships have lasted to this day, even after I moved to another city. The day I left, the entire group went with me to the bus station, not letting me go without photos and chocolates and handwritten letters and kisses and hugs and many encouraging words.

I didn't die of thirst in the desert of Monterrey after all. I drank from delicious wells I never would have found if it hadn't been for Jesus. He taught me how to treat others, copying and pasting the love I wish I had. What will happen when you take the initiative—the same initiative that Christ took with you?

ELEVEN
THE TASTE OF REJECTION
AND DIEGO'S PROMISE

Diego stood, waiting for the bus. He had finally gotten out of school for the day. He wanted to get as far away as he could from that place and those little jerks. Good thing he didn't live close by. Cornfields and meadows separated his house from the small town. But if his mom had listened to him, Diego would have increased that distance by 414 miles. He would have moved back to Monterrey in a heartbeat.

Why did they have to leave? It was a question and a complaint at the same time. His mom had uprooted him from Monterrey, where he'd been with all his friends—Monterrey, home of soccer champions; Monterrey, a city with metros and universities; Monterrey, famous for barbecues and skyscrapers. And now Diego found himself among grazing cows.

It was the first day of middle school in the town of Doctor Mora, Guanajuato. Diego entered the classroom. His hair was gelled back, his smile whiter than vanilla ice cream. (Nowadays I think if he doesn't get a job as a lawyer, his surefire Plan B should be modeling for H&M.) All heads turned to see him pass by. And for a moment, Diego felt like a rock star. Maybe this cultured young man from civilization had made a good impression?

He sat at his desk, and the lesson began. After a few minutes, Diego looked away from the teacher to contemplate his new kingdom. It wasn't long before he saw his classmates' eyes. They weren't filled with admiration. Squinted and tense, they seemed to be shooting lasers at him like Cyclops from the X-Men.

At eleven years of age, Diego became acquainted with the taste of rejection: bitter. It's a cocktail as icy as the backs his classmates turned on him. And it's intoxicating too, because they left my friend more confused than ever. Were they jealous of Diego? Maybe he'd aroused their defensive instinct for their town? Why the heck were they treating him like this? For the first time in his life, Diego was the target of insults. As kids do best, they twisted his name into all kinds of embarrassing nicknames.

So there was Diego standing at the bus stop, already sick of the rejection he'd been served, when a short kid walked up. At school, he was all jokes. He had singled Diego out in front of everyone. But, surprise surprise, he kept to himself at the bus stop. To Diego, his very presence felt repulsive.

Diego whirled around, and before the boy could register what was happening, he was on his back on the ground with my friend on his chest. "Don't mess with me, you hear?" And like a comet from space, his fist crashed against the kid's face. The crater it left that day wasn't any physical wound. It was worse than that. It was complete distrust between Diego and the kids of the town.

AT THE PACE GLACIERS MELT INTO STREAMS, THINGS STARTED to flow for Diego. He was now fourteen and had managed to make a few friends in Doctor Mora. These were the kids who lived nearby. They would explore the fields together on their bikes and watch TV in the heat of the afternoons.

And something else was new. One day, his mom took him to a Christian church. They went through the doors into what seemed like a parallel universe. It was a place where people smiled. Their hugs and kisses were more than formalities; they were showing real affection. They prayed as though God heard them. They treated each other as though they cared for one another. With time, Diego concluded that his first impression of the church had been the reality.

I remember when I was Diego's age. Ah, adolescence. I awoke to many realities. Like deodorant. And the fact that girls didn't have cooties. During that period, I felt an emptiness in me for the first time—like I was desperately missing something. Before then, if I had a need, it could be met. Like when you change a baby's diaper or you give him a toy, he calms down. But this sense of something missing in my life felt like nothing I'd ever experienced.

Where I came from, snowboarding was synonymous with cool. If you had a board, you were immortal—like those guys we idolized in video games. And it turned out I was a natural at bombing down ski slopes. But I felt this drive in me to jump higher, ride faster, and let people see how good I was, as if these things would somehow fill the empty place inside me.

People have all sorts of ways to try to fill their empty places. During adolescence, a lot of teens try marijuana. Those years are also when some have their first sexual experiences. Doing these things, they are trying to extinguish in their flesh what is burning in their spirit.

But it was different for Diego. He had a refuge greater than those distractions. He had a more potent relief than substances. Diego made the decision to know the Christ that the people at his church knew. Diego turned to Him.

His friends heard about it. Would they share this excitement like they had when they'd gathered around the TV and their favorite movie came on? Would they be curious about his decision with the same curiosity they had for the animals they discovered in the countryside?

Actually, no. Diego now seemed weird to them, like he wasn't who they'd thought he was. Maybe it was their parents who didn't let them play with him anymore, but for whatever reason, Diego once again found himself all alone. His bike sat leaning against the side of his house. His TV set felt depressing now.

Sometimes when Diego couldn't take it anymore, he locked himself in the bathroom to vent his frustration. In tears, he questioned God, "Why does this always happen to me? Why? Where are You, God?"

JESUS HAS A POLARIZING EFFECT. WHEN YOU MEET HIM— when you encounter His words and His power—you don't stay the same. Either you love Him or He is repulsive to you.

Those who love Him have served other masters: dreams of success in their careers, chasing after a blissful family experience, ambition to accomplish something great, other gods. But these masters turned out to be cruel. They promised happiness but never delivered. In Christ, though, these people found a gentle and good King.

Those repulsed by Jesus cannot imagine Him taking preeminence in their lives. Would He dethrone their dreams? Would His agenda supersede theirs? Would they let Him dictate what right and wrong is? Would they wait on Him for their reward? All of it sounds outrageous to them.

It hurts the most when that second kind of person is someone close to you—someone you love. Ever since Jesus came, even families have been polarized.

> Whoever loves father or mother more than me is not worthy
> of me, and whoever loves son or daughter more than me is
> not worthy of me. And whoever does not take his cross and

follow me is not worthy of me. Whoever finds his life will lose it, and whoever loses his life for my sake will find it. (Matthew 10:37–39)

So the follower of Christ finds himself between a rock and a hard place. You love and honor your friends with a renewed tenderness. At the same time, you love God with everything you are. These loves shouldn't be exclusive, but some people will give you an ultimatum: "Me or God."

That kind of ultimatum makes me think: *Who knitted me in my mother's womb? Who formed the constellations but is so close that He knows my intimate thoughts?* The creativity of my artistic friends inspires me, but if I have to choose between their paintings of the sunrise and the sunrise itself, I know which one I'll choose. If I have to choose between the Creator and creation, I know which one I'll choose. If I have to decide between loves, I know the love that people give sometimes burns with passion but often goes out altogether.

A friend can encourage you to get better, but no one can cure the cancer of sin in your soul. Doctors have discovered what is good for your health, but nobody can stop the decay of death in you. Only God resurrects the dead.

If they make me choose, I know Who I'll choose.

Even so, there is nothing like the warmth of a hug or meeting someone's gaze. It's for this reason that Jesus gave us a promise:

And he said to them, "Truly, I say to you, there is no one who has left house or wife or brothers or parents or children, for the sake of the kingdom of God, who will not receive many times more in this time, and in the age to come eternal life." (Luke 18:29–30)

I met Diego when he was in college. He had managed to return to Monterrey, the city he'd so reluctantly left. He was one of the friends I made at a taco outing. We got along well. He expressed himself with his hands and facial gestures. If you transcribed his dialogues, there would be a lot of exclamation points. I was new to the city, and he could tell. He invited me to his grandparents' house to watch the soccer games of the local favorite: Los Tigres. He sent me texts to ask how I was doing. And at Easter, he invited me to Doctor Mora.

Perhaps you're imagining our entrance to Doctor Mora like the entrances of cowboys in old Western movies: Tumbleweeds rolling in the distance. The wind whistling. A revolver in each hand. Eyes alert for any bandidos on the streets.

But it wasn't like that. Imagine instead the homecoming of a war hero. While we walked down the main street, people greeted us from the shops. We heard "Hola, Diego" from a car that passed by. We saw a hand in the air waving at us from the main plaza. I wondered for a minute if my friend was the mayor of the town.

I'd expected to stay in his mother's house, but Diego had so many people he wanted to see. We ended up sleeping in the homes of three different families. If my count is correct, we have sat in the living rooms of eight different families in all our visits to Mora. One of them has a temazcal, a kind of a sauna. Who would have thought sitting and sweating could be such fun?

It seems like wherever we travel, Diego has someone to stay with: Querétaro, La Sierra Gorda, Monterrey, Doctor Mora, Ciudad de Guanajuato, Zacatecas, Sonora, Ciudad de México, Morelia, and, of course, Portland, Oregon. As densely as the rows of corn grow around his house, friends surround Diego.

I WONDER, WHAT MADE THE DIFFERENCE FOR MY FRIEND? WHY was he hated as a kid but beloved as a young man? Maybe it's because life with Christ is the natural environment for friendship. Read the following statements and ask yourself: *Would friendship grow there?*

> Love your neighbor as yourself. (Mark 12:31)
> Love your enemies and pray for those who persecute you. (Matthew 5:44)
> Blessed are the peacemakers. (Matthew 5:9)
> Give to everyone who begs from you, and from one who takes away your goods do not demand them back. (Luke 6:30)

This certainly is fertile ground.

Maybe Diego had so many friends because he had stopped seeing life as a victim. When the seed of friendship falls on a victim's field, it dries up because he carries a machete for self-defense instead of a hose for watering.

While these are my theories, if you ask Diego what changed everything, he points to something else. He says God didn't give him the escape he wanted back in junior high; rather, what God gave him was a promise: "There is no one who has left house or wife or brothers or parents or children, for the sake of the kingdom of God, who will not receive many times more" (Luke 18:29–30).

And my friend dared to believe it.

TWELVE

LET YOUR YES BE YES

ABOUT LIES AND TOMORROW

A food stand sat in front of my apartment in Monterrey. The family who ran it sold local favorites—the majority of which are *deep* deep-fried.

One night, I went down to order *flautas* (they're basically rolled-up tacos). While the potatoes and meat were frying, I went into observation mode. The stand was a card table with a frier and some ingredient containers. The family had set up some folding chairs on the sidewalk. The mother cooked, and the father chatted with customers waiting for their orders. On the ground, a three-year-old sat and played. Behind them, a baby cooed in its carriage.

That night, an older man was with them. His easy way with the family and his tenderness with the kids made me think he was their grandfather. As Dad told jokes and Mom cooked, their three-year-old began to roam away from the stand. Alert to what was happening, Grandpa called out to the child: "Son, come back. There's a mean dog over there."

I looked down the street to try to locate this dangerous beast.

At the same time, Mom looked up from the plates to see

her wandering boy. "Yes, son," she said. "Come right now. It's reeeeeeaally mean. Run along!"

Soon enough, the child came back to the safety of his parents.

A happy ending, right?

If every story has a moral, what is the one this child has learned? That it's always good to have Grandpa watching over you? That at a certain distance from your parents, wild animals are waiting to pounce on you?

Sooner or later, the boy is going to discover the reality—or lack thereof—of the "mean dogs." The moral he will learn is that you can lie to control others.

This incident seemed strange to me—until I eventually saw the sequel, the trilogy, and the spin-off with other families. Then I realized lying was a whole genre of child-raising. One mother got her little daughter to come to her with bait: "Come here, and I'll give you a piece of candy." She had no such candy. In a restaurant, a father wanted his son to eat his food instead of playing with it, so he threatened him: "Son, eat up. If you don't... look, that man over there will take you away." After my school's activities, I sometimes have to wait with students until their parents pick them up. "I'm almost there" or "I'm two blocks away" means there will be at least another twenty-minute delay.

Why do parents turn to lies? I guess it's the easy way out. Molding a little human's character is arduous work that takes years, but if you lie to them, you get instant results.

THESE PARENTS DON'T UNDERSTAND A FUNDAMENTAL REALITY: if you choose a lie today, you sacrifice the truth tomorrow.

When my friends remember their childhood, the lie that most disillusioned them was this: "I'll buy it for you tomorrow." Have you heard that one? A kid will ask for something on a whim, something usually made of pure sugar, something that goes beyond their parents' budget. Instead of saying "No," his mom says, "Tomorrow."

Tomorrow starts when the sun's rays cross the horizon and night turns to day. We can calculate with scientific precision just when *tomorrow* comes. All you need is a clock. If today the kid's mother says "Tomorrow," he can believe that the following day they are going to return to that store. It can't mean anything else.

Right?

The satirical author Mariano José de Larra wrote about this phenomenon.[1] In his famous essay "Vuelva Usted Mañana" ("Come Back Tomorrow"), a fictitious foreigner goes to Spain to do some paperwork, a process that in his country of origin typically takes ten days.

Exasperated and exhausted, the foreigner eventually gives up. "After six months, I haven't accomplished anything except to be told 'Come back tomorrow,' and when this blessed 'tomorrow' finally comes, they tell me flat-out 'No'?"

Like screws stripped by use, all meaning is stripped away from this word by lie after lie. *Tomorrow* becomes useless. But the word is stuck, drilled into the minds of children. As it rusts, the only thing *tomorrow* means is that promises are never kept.

Larra concludes: "Woe to that tomorrow that never ever comes!"

We've seen Larra's thoughts on the topic of lies, but what does God think about it? Let's go to the Scriptures:

Now if Christ is proclaimed as raised from the dead, how can some of you say that there is no resurrection of the dead? But if there is no resurrection of the dead, then not even Christ has been raised. (1 Corinthians 15:12–13)

Why is the apostle Paul making such a fuss about this? The Corinthians seem to have their ideas about life and death, and he has his. Isn't a plurality of opinions welcome?

Not when it comes to the truth. Christianity is based on truth claims. When the Bible narrates the worldwide flood or the ten plagues of Egypt, it is referring to historical events. They might be factual, or they might be myths. The claims are either accurate or erroneous.

> And if Christ has not been raised, then our preaching is in vain and your faith is in vain. We are even found to be misrepresenting God, because we testified about God that he raised Christ, whom he did not raise if it is true that the dead are not raised. (1 Corinthians 15:14–15)

So, Christianity makes truth claims, but if it turns out they are lies, then huge implications follow. If you take out the steel beams, the whole building comes crashing down. Standing in the rubble of a false religion, Paul would wonder: *Why should we preach?* I think it follows to add: *Why should we sing praises? Why should we read the Bible? What benefit beyond socializing would congregating in a church give us?*

> For if the dead are not raised, not even Christ has been raised. And if Christ has not been raised, your faith is futile and you are still in your sins. Then those also who have fallen asleep in Christ have perished. If in Christ we have hope in this life only, we are of all people most to be pitied. (1 Corinthians 15:16–19)

"We are of all people most to be pitied." Strong words, right? The American philosopher Thomas Nagel wrote about this situation. As an atheist, he would classify Christianity and its claims as at best, false; at worst, lies. Therefore, he doesn't believe there is a resurrection from the dead.

Contemplating death, Nagel knows his degrees from Cornell, Oxford, and Harvard won't help him at the end of his days. His decades on Planet Earth, just a particle in the universe, don't add up to anything compared to the infinite time that will follow him. The books and articles he wrote will disintegrate in a sea of forgetfulness.

That's why Nagel concludes, "Life may be not only meaningless but absurd."[2]

IF YOUR ETERNAL DESTINY DEPENDS ON BELIEVING JESUS AND His promises, shouldn't honesty matter to you? Shouldn't you be a man or woman of your word?

If that is your conviction, Jesus shows us the way: "But let your 'Yes' be 'Yes,' and your 'No,' 'No.' For whatever is more than these is from the evil one" (Matthew 5:37 NKJV).

This is blessed simplicity. What you say, you do. When people get to know you, they see that appearances and reality are the same. They can let down their guard around you. They can make plans with you. They can make deals with you. It simplifies everything.

What isn't so simple is *keeping* your word.

After living in Monterrey for a year, I moved south to the city of Morelia, Michoacán, to work as a teacher at an organization called NOE International. That's where I met Calvin.

He was a big boy for his age, and his personality was XXL. He often greeted me by yelling from far off, and he did it in English.

Calvin always had some mischievous plan in motion. One time, he showed off his new toy for me. He gave it to me to hold while I answered a riddle. When I didn't get the right answer, the toy gave me an electric shock! Another day, apparently bored of that prank, Calvin mobilized all the little kids on that street to play a game. I didn't catch what they were doing, but through the window, I could hear Calvin changing the rules of the game to his benefit on multiple occasions.

A certain day, Calvin asked me for Cheetos. At first, it rubbed me the wrong way that he'd ask me so bluntly like that. I was locking up the school, and I turned the key slowly to think about my response. *Of course I don't have a bag of Cheetos in my back pocket. And I'm not going to give him money. No.*

But, Andrew, what if he's really hungry? This is an opportunity to show him love. An opportunity.

I turned around and smiled at him. "Of course, Calvin. I'm going to run an errand, and I'll come back with some Cheetos. Can you wait for me here? I'll be fifteen minutes."

I walked five blocks to pick up an order of sushi. That night, some friends were going to visit my house to have dinner. I began to think about the chores I had to do before they came, and, carried away by that train of thought, I completely forgot about the Cheetos.

I headed homeward for about fifteen minutes. Halfway there, I saw a convenience store. The memory struck me like lightning: *Calvin!* I went in and bought a bag of Cheetos.

I doubled back and almost ran to the school. I had said fifteen minutes, but by now, forty had passed. *Don't leave, Calvin. I'm coming! Once again,* I thought, *someone makes a promise to him and doesn't keep it. He's going to think I told him what I did just to get rid of him.*

I turned the corner, and the school was now in sight. On the steps in front of the entrance sat Calvin. I thanked God and went up to him. The two of us sat down for a while to chat and eat our snack. I was elated for the extended opportunity to make my "yes" a "yes."

In the quarantine of 2020, I did something I don't normally do: I met my neighbors. It was incredible! Mrs. Lidia invited me to her house to try her recipes. I met her kids, ten-year-old Nahomi and eight-year-old Emiliano. Soon I found myself in their house almost every day because I was giving one-on-one English lessons to Nahomi.

Lidia was delighted with the situation. Her kids had spent months hardly seeing anyone, and cabin fever had set in. But now morale was changing. She shared with me that Emiliano had said my roommate Felipe and I were his my best friends in the whole world. There are a lot of countries out there filled with billions of potential friends, but making moments with him over Legos rushed us to the top of the list.

One day, Lidia invited me to have dinner with her family later that week. I said, "Yes, I'd love to come."

On Friday afternoon, my friend Grant and I were in the garage working on a project when Emiliano came out to greet us. He asked if I was going to come to the dinner party that night. I said, "Yes, it's going to be a fun time," and turned my attention back to the project.

Emiliano added, "Eight o'clock, okay?"

"Yep, see you at eight."

He began to talk about his favorite video game, but then a more urgent idea came to his mind. He interrupted himself, "But you're for sure going to come, right?"

"Definitely. I'll be there."

In the course of ten minutes, Emiliano must have gotten a dozen RSVPs out of me.

Afterward, I wondered why this had just happened. I supposed that even at his young age, Emiliano had already learned not to get his hopes up when someone promised him something, especially if it was something he wanted badly.

At eight o'clock, I knocked on my neighbor's door. Emiliano opened it up, and instead of greeting me, he ran around the living room. He was like a balloon inflated to the max that just couldn't hold in its excitement anymore, so it went flying in circles. Suddenly, he charged at me and gave me a huge hug.

"It's so good to see you, Andrew!"

After a night of pizza and chatting, Lidia leaned over and told me that Emiliano had been running a countdown in his head all day.

Honestly, it isn't often that people welcome me with high-intensity happiness like that. It's not every day that a person experiences that kind of euphoria just from being in the presence of another.

I hope Emiliano never loses that. I hope he always lives with a sense of expectation. And I wish the same for you. So here's something you can look forward to: at the end of days, God will gather His people together and be with us. Like the apostle Paul wrote, we'll see Christ resurrected and glorious. The letdowns, the unfulfilled promises, the false hopes, and every *no* will be swept away with death itself. We'll see His *yes* was really *yes*, and *tomorrow* has finally come.

THIRTEEN
BUY FRIENDSHIP
YOUR BEST INVESTMENT

The child stopped playing. He left the action figure on the grass in front of his house and stood to listen to the roar of an engine. Suddenly, a Mercedes-Benz rushed past him at highway speeds. With a screech of its tires, the vehicle rounded the corner and disappeared into the residential neighborhood.

The car slammed on its brakes and skidded into a driveway. A man got out, marched toward the modern house, and threw the door open. Inside, he loosened his silk tie and threw his jacket on the sofa. He began to pace the living room, mumbling to himself.

His reputation at work had been destroyed. He was now blacklisted. No one in the industry would hire Manuel Peña after this. What was he going to do? He looked at his hands; they were soft and adorned with three gold rings. He wasn't going to become a bricklayer, that was for sure. He imagined himself at an intersection walking up to cars to wash their windshields for spare change. He laughed to himself for a moment, then stopped. He would never do that. He just needed two seconds to think. *Think!*

An hour before, Manuel had been sitting in a high-backed

leather chair in a company conference room. He hadn't been expecting the ambush: in front of his boss, he was accused of embezzlement. He was fired in that same meeting, and now he had to turn in his books with the company accounts tomorrow at nine.

The worst part was the accusation had been true. Manuel was a magician: there was sleight of hand in every deal. And now he would have to pay for it all. But maybe, he thought, he could pull off one more trick. He grabbed his briefcase and jacket and ran back to his Mercedes. He had eighteen hours, and the clock was running.

"So I see here you owe three hundred forty thousand to the business," said Manuel to a man on the other side of the desk.

"Yes, that's right, but as per the contract, there is a repayment term of—"

"I know what the contract says," Manuel cut him off, smiling. "I wrote it, remember? Relax. I'm not here to ask you for anything." Manuel leaned back in his chair and crossed his legs. "Actually, I see you as a highly valued client. I'm here today with a show of gratitude. What do you say we lower that pending debt to two hundred thousand?"

The other man hesitated a moment, tried to read Manuel. When there was apparently no catch to this offer, a smile spread across his face. "Well, umm... Manuel, thanks. Seriously."

Manuel took a pen and a new contract out of his briefcase, saying, "This is how I treat my friends."

The man nodded. "Friends." He took the pen to sign the paper.

After filing the sheet, Manuel stood to go.

At this, the other man offered, "Manuel, if you need anything, don't hesitate to call me, you know? Anything."

Manuel furrowed his eyebrows and nodded his head.

"That's thoughtful of you." He shrugged and said, "Well, maybe I'll take you up on that one of these days."

Minutes later, the Mercedes-Benz flew down the highway. He had sixteen hours left until he had to turn in the accounts. The modifications had to be made right now. He hurried from one appointment to the next with his old clients, lowering their debts to the company. As the hours passed, Manuel accumulated more favors. Soon he would cash them in. This was Manuel's way of not losing the luxurious life he'd gotten used to.

THIS STORY IS A CONTEMPORARY VERSION OF A PARABLE IN THE Bible. Jesus told fictitious stories to illustrate the points he was making. The first time I read this parable, I thought, *They're going to catch this rat. They're going to throw him in jail, or even better, since this is the Roman era, they'll flog him.*

I hurried up to read the end: "The master commended the dishonest manager because he had acted shrewdly" (Luke 16:8 NIV).

What! That's how it ends? Jesus makes up a crooked protagonist and lets him win?

That's right, Jesus replies with a wink. *But calm down, it's just a story. Don't let the point of it escape you:*

> For the people of this world are more shrewd in dealing with their own kind than are the people of the light. I tell you, use worldly wealth to gain friends for yourselves, so that when it is gone, you will be welcomed into eternal dwellings. (Luke 16:8–9 NIV)

Let's pay attention to the words "worldly wealth." Who talks about money like that? We live in the world, so it's logical to think of all wealth as worldly, but we don't walk around saying "worldly mangoes," "worldly beaches," or "worldly art." The specification of "worldly" is not necessary because these things are only found on this planet and in this life.

And that's where Jesus makes us question, "Or are they?" Is it true that the riches you have today are the only riches that exist?

Then Jesus said, "when it is gone." He didn't say, "in case it runs out" or "if it runs out." He said, "*when.*" Maybe you'll arrive at your tomb with millions, but you won't take your wealth any further. The riches you have are only in your possession for a short time. The clock is running.

What Jesus appreciated about the crooked manager is that this man realized the urgency of his situation. Obligated to decide what mattered most, he opted for friends.

For friends. Was it a good choice? He invested in friendship because it would last longer than the salary from his job. But you and I aren't conniving employees (I hope), so what will last longer for us? Let's see, companies eventually capitulate and get replaced. Artistic masterpieces deteriorate and are forgotten. Pyramids are subject to wear and erosion. Nowadays we know that not even the stars escape death. Few things last for eternity, but this parable identifies two of them: people and the relationships we build with them.

Putting the pieces of Jesus's argument together, if you want to use your fleeting resources to make a difference for eternity, you have to *buy friendship.*

I WASN'T THE ONLY ONE LEFT PERPLEXED BY THIS PARABLE. IN Colombia, my friend Claudia once opened her Bible to the same passage.

One afternoon, Claudia and her sister returned home from the gym. There's nothing like coming home at the end of the day, especially if you have a lovely place. They had a living room with warm lighting and modern furniture; a bathroom with artistic tile work. Between the two bedrooms was an office with a desk and bookshelves full of legal books. The office was where Claudia worked.

The sisters had decorated the house with an eye for details, but having it kept clean and orderly was the finishing touch— thanks to their domestic employee, Rocío. When they came home that day and saw Rocío washing dishes, they greeted her like always. But they saw someone else in the house Claudia hadn't been expecting: a baby.

The child was sitting on the floor, and she smiled up at Claudia when they came in. The baby's outfit wasn't "divine," as upscale women say, not like the children in magazines. *Oh no!* thought Claudia. *This baby is going to scream and throw fits.* Claudia needed quiet to write her documents. It was fine for Rocío to work here but not for her to bring people into her house. Claudia gave Rocío and the child a half-smile and went to her office.

Now alone, Claudia opened her laptop to start her work. She signed in, but her fingers hovered over the keyboard. She stared at the screen, unable to concentrate. She closed the laptop. Her conscience was speaking to her.

Just then, her half-closed door swung partly open, and baby Laurita peeked in. She crawled into the room. She locked eyes with Claudia like only babies can. The young professional stood and gathered the baby off the floor. She kissed her on the forehead. Hugging her, she caressed her button nose and expressive eyebrows. Claudia carried Laurita back into the kitchen to her mom.

Once again in her office, Claudia broke down in tears. The Holy Spirit had revealed to her what was happening in her heart. In her own words:

> I rejected her due to a deep elitism, which I had suffered from ever since my cultural formation in which I never learned to relate intimately with poor people. It was painful

for me to realize something so ugly was reigning in my heart.

Since I had learned that Jesus doesn't condemn me for my mistakes but rather helps me overcome them when I expose them sincerely in prayer, I went to my office to cry to Him, confessing this sin I had in my heart. He showed me the root of my sin, made me feel His forgiveness, and showed me a strategy to leave that condition.

That strategy was the same one the crooked manager used: buying friendship. Claudia decided to invest in Rocío and Laurita. In the beginning, my friend gave them what is often the hardest to sacrifice: her time. When Laurita came crawling into the office, Claudia closed the project on her laptop to give her some affection. Laurita would sit on Claudia's lap to listen to children's songs on the computer. The two of them sang together—their favorites were Alex Campos's songs.

After a few months, Claudia decided to invest more in them. Since Rocío was raising her daughter alone, working, and studying on top of that, Claudia had an idea. She could take Laurita one Saturday so Rocío could study without distraction.

And so my friend got on the TransMilenio, Bogotá's public transport to make the hour-and-a-half journey south. As she went, she looked through the windows and saw fewer fancy boutiques and more graffiti. The open-air restaurants with umbrellas and hanging lights were replaced with carts selling street food. It didn't matter that she was going to the part of town where gangsters and paramilitary units ran the streets, because that was where her friends lived. Claudia did hold her cell phone a little tighter, though.

When the doors of the TransMilenio opened, there standing and waiting for her were Laurita and Rocío. When the child saw Claudia, she started to hop and smile. This was the beginning of their Saturday adventure.

It was a sugary whirlwind of fun. They rowed canoes in an amusement park, they ate ice cream, and they laughed a lot. The big finish of the afternoon was their visit to the church El Lugar de Su Presencia.

Maybe Laurita wouldn't remember the details of that day, as she was only two, but the message of the day would be etched in the little girl forever: *Claudia loves me, and so does her God.*

It was so much fun, why shouldn't they do it again? Claudia picked up the little child each week. They did the things girls love, especially shopping. They bought cute bows, "divine" shoes, and anything wearable and pink! Together they became fashionistas. They also explored places to eat. When I visited Claudia, she took me to an ice cream shop where they made the ice cream in front of us, freezing the cream with the ingredients we had chosen. These Saturday escapes with Laurita continued for years.

If you get to know my friend, soon you'll realize she thinks far beyond fashion. She contemplates the future. It occurred to Claudia she could provide Laurita with an education.

With this intention, she signed her up at a kindergarten called Sueños de Colores (Colorful Dreams). When I saw it, I wondered whether it was a kindergarten school or Disneyland. The gate that surrounded the kindergarten was made of giant colored pencils that looked like they had materialized out of a cartoon. On both sides of the sign were 3-D cartoon children painting. Paintbrushes the size of trees marked the entrance. My friend didn't want to send Laurita to any old school.

Claudia reflected on those days: "As I did this act of obedience to Jesus, my heart was changing to the point of loving this girl as if she were my own daughter." As such, Claudia included Laurita in her family vacations. They flew to the coastal Caribbean city of Cartagena and to Colombia's coffee-growing region. In Barranquilla, Laurita met Claudia's parents. They loved on her as if they were her grandparents.

Laurita grew up. She became a voracious reader, and do you know what she likes to read? Her Bible. An analytic girl, she tells her classmates at school that Jesus exists and is good. She even asks Claudia and her sister to buy Bibles so she can give them to her little friends. Do you think Claudia hesitates one second before saying yes to this request? Of course not! Laurita also learned to dream big because she knows that she has no limits with God. She wants to study in France to become an architect so she can build a house for her mom.

A house would be nice, but they have a home now. Rocío got married a few years ago to a good man. Today they are building their family on the foundation of Christ.

I'M HAPPY FOR LAURITA AND HER FAMILY; THEY GOT THE storybook ending. But what about Claudia? She could have used that time and money on herself. Do you ever find yourself saying something like this: *If I'm generous with people, what will be left for me?* To this, Jesus replies, *People! And what you'll gain you can never lose.*

As if eternity weren't enough, God throws in something for now as well. Here is how Claudia concludes:

> The result of this experience was that my heart became sensitive to the needs of people. I learned that for God there are no rich or poor people, only souls that Jesus loves deeply. He wants to transform their lives, blessing them and giving them opportunities that surpass their expectations. He changes their future of curses to a future of blessings.

FOURTEEN

THE "GIVE IT ALL AWAY GAMBIT"

IT'S YOUR MOVE

The young man's brown eyes wandered. He didn't say a word, but he couldn't hide his intense internal dialogue. He had just been offered exactly what he wanted, but his face fell. Slowly, he turned to go home empty-handed.

We all want something. We would like to finish our degree. We want to travel. We have dream cars and bucket lists. We have unsaid words and un-lost weight. Desire is the air we breathe.

But when you put a price on something, you discover not all desires are the same. Some people empty their bank accounts to get the thing they want. Some people get up early to go to the gym and stay up late studying. But other people, like this unhappy young man, consider the price and decide not to pay it.

Now, this young man wasn't a rude person. He had pious parents who had raised him up with morals. He had a good work ethic. What's more, he had respect for others. You could see this when he spoke with Jesus: the young man showed Him honor by kneeling down.

There's one more thing this young man had. It wasn't a

character quality but a thing—lots of things, actually. He was fantastically rich.

And what was it he wanted? A selfie with the famous prophet? A heavenly blessing on his business's new location? A keynote speaker for his next conference? No, he didn't want any superficial thing. This man went to the heart of what Jesus offers: he wanted to know how he could inherit eternal life.

Look how Jesus responded:

> And Jesus, looking at him, loved him, and said to him, "You lack one thing: go, sell all that you have and give to the poor, and you will have treasure in heaven; and come, follow me." (Mark 10:21)

It's not that everyone ought to become homeless, and it isn't a virtue to earn less than anyone else. But this is what Jesus told this wealthy man to do. Like Morpheus in *The Matrix*, Jesus offered the man two open hands, one with the blue pill and one with the red pill. Jesus gave him the opportunity to choose eternal life or riches. "Disheartened by the saying, he went away sorrowful, for he had great possessions" (Mark 10:22).

The eternal destiny of this man wasn't a question of whether he was a decent person, because he was; it was a question of what he treasured.

Jesus doesn't ask everyone to rid themselves of all their possessions, but he does give a paradoxical teaching that applies to everyone:

> Then Jesus told his disciples, "If anyone would come after me, let him deny himself and take up his cross and follow me. For whoever would save his life will lose it, but whoever loses his life for my sake will find it." (Matthew 16:24–25)

And there it is: this story's ledge. Let me tell you about a friend who took the step forward off of it.

THERE IS A PLACE IN BOGOTÁ, COLOMBIA, WHERE PEOPLE ride bicycles in expansive parks, where you can find professional dog walkers on redbrick sidewalks, where people have breakfast in chic cafés. That's where my friend Claudia lived —the young woman you met in the previous chapter.

Although she had her dream life there, she decided to leave it to see what else God had in store for her. She bought a ticket and flew north, to Mexico. There she studied theology as an intern for a year at a church called Más Vida. As her practicum, she visited small churches in forgotten corners of Michoacán to support them in their ministries.

She was and still is a missionary. Different than many missionaries, she supports herself. Thanks to the Internet, she does her job as a lawyer from her apartment in Morelia.

Now I'll give the microphone to Claudia. She'll narrate the story, and I'll just interrupt every once in a while.

When I arrived for the first time at Morelia, I went to a Sunday service at church. In the middle of worship, God prompted me to give an offering equivalent to all the money I was counting on for my expenses those first days, including what I would have spent that Sunday.

Does this sound familiar? She looked at the metaphorical game board, and it was her turn. God had once again played the "give it all away" gambit.

I'm not entirely sure, but my theory is that all of us at some point will have the opportunity to turn our faith into action by giving away all we have. Brad, my Spanish teacher, had recently married and was living abroad in England when his turn came. He and his wife had four thousand dollars in their bank account, and in one fell swoop, they donated it. A widow living through a famine used the last of her flour and oil to make a meal for the prophet Elijah (1 Kings 17). Get ready, because your turn might come soon.

> The thought of daring to do what God was asking me scared me. It meant that from the moment I put that envelope in the offering box, I wouldn't have any money, not even to eat. What's more, before the service I had promised my friend, a fellow foreigner, that I'd take her out to eat after the church service.

Let me tell you that Claudia isn't someone who goes around with nothing to buy food. I know because she hosted me when I visited Colombia. Thanks to generosity you usually only see in movies, we drank cold-brew nitro coffee and ate pounds of fine cuts of beef and sushi prepared by chefs in white uniforms. So her decision to give it all away fell way outside her comfort zone.

> Jesus's invitation to make an offering created a conflict in my mind, so I decided to ignore the idea as though it were a product of my imagination. But since the Holy Spirit doesn't ignore anything, He kept bringing this idea to mind while I was worshipping.
>
> He reminded me of the days prior to my trip to Mexico. He told me this new experience in my life would make me trust Him more and know Him like never before, that there were greater levels of faith than those I had experienced up to now. He wanted me to climb up those steps. Finally, I couldn't resist so many arguments, so I decided to put my envelope in the offering box before I could change my mind again.

That's how I understand what Jesus told the wealthy young man. Far from being motivated by a whim, "Jesus, looking at him, loved him." In love, Christ was inviting him to the next level of faith. Because when your money meets all your needs, a question gets lodged in your mind: *Is God the One who takes care of me, or is it me? Theoretically, I believe God is present in my life, but how can I know for sure?* When your needs are provided for in such a way that you know God is responsible for it, you discover who He is. I think Christ wanted this rich young man to know Him.

When the meeting ended, the pastor presented the group of us internship students to the congregation. In a joking tone, he told everyone to greet us, take us out to eat, and give us money.

A lady came up to me. I didn't know her at the time. She said she was so happy about what I had decided to do for God, and she felt God had put it on her heart to give me something. She gave me an envelope. I couldn't hide my awestruck wonder when I found in it the same amount I had just given as an offering for missions. I wanted to cry!

In this way, Jesus taught me His faithfulness and the precision of His words when He said He would take care of our needs as we invest in His kingdom.

Not content with that, Jesus went beyond what I could expect in fulfillment of that promise. The following week, the woman who had given me an offering also left a book for me in the church's café. It was a book on leadership.

Because the topic of the book didn't seem attractive to me at that time, I left it on my bookshelf for a few months without even thumbing through the pages. But a time came when I had a crisis of leadership and needed to learn more about it. Asking the Lord to show me how to learn about the topic, He reminded me I had a book on my shelf.

When I opened it to see its contents, I found a thousand

pesos inside it, left by the woman from church. With them was a note saying the money was for a time when I had a financial need. Just that week, I had expenses that went beyond my normal monthly budget.

This was another surprise that made my faith in Jesus and His unlimited love for me grow. He always cares for every detail of my life, and He goes before the circumstances of my life.

AN EXPERIENCE OF LOVE. A CLOSER BOND OF TRUST WITH HER Creator. Optimism about the future. I don't know what that sounds like to you, but to me, it sounds like an abundant life, a foretaste of eternal life. This is what the rich young man went looking for. Maybe he never knew it, but the heaven we are waiting for can tear open the curtains of today and bathe us in its light.

And that is worth any price.

FIFTEEN
WHEN YOU STUMBLE UPON TREASURE
ON LOSSES AND GAINS

A couple of bare light bulbs hung from cables in an improvised canopy. Just within the reach of its light, people stood in a circle. If you looked, you could make out the dress jackets and ties of businessmen, the sweat-stained sombreros of farmers, and the tattooed arms of delinquents. Shadows distorted the features of their faces. It looked like the darkness of the jungle outside was reaching its claws around them.

One of the people in the circle barely rose to the height of everyone else's shoulders—a boy in junior high. He had black hair combed back with gel and a shirt with various buttons open.

In the middle of the circle, under the light, two men carried roosters and showed them to the audience. The boy offered a bet to the person next to him, a man dressed in a tracksuit. This heavyset man looked at the boy from head to foot with silent reproach.

But the boy didn't back down. His ancestors were Aztec warriors. You could see it in bronze skin and square jaw; you could see it in his attitude. He was hard to dismiss, so the man accepted his bet.

After putting sharpened razors on the roosters' legs, the

trainers lifted these rival animals so they could see each other
—a kind of barnyard face-off—and then they were let loose
on the ground.

The clandestine cockfight had begun.

The roosters lunged at one another and collided. It was
like a pillow fight, feathers flying as they scrambled about. The
heavy man interlaced his fingers and leaned forward. His
breathing accelerated as the fight unfolded below. He threw a
glance at the boy. He was eating some tacos and licking a
finger, nonchalant. This lad had already seen everything at
cockfights: drunks who bet their houses and losers who pulled
out revolvers.

The rooster on the green side dove headfirst on top of the
other. It gave a peck to the immobile lump that was its oppo-
nent, its back a sticky clump of feathers and blood. A knowing
smile spread across the face of the boy. The fight was almost
over.

Just then, the people heard a heavy sound. It came from
the darkness outside the tent. The noise was like a cyclical
growl. Pairs of parallel light beams passed through the underbrush like sword thrusts. The diesel roar was unmistakable:
the army was coming.

For raids like this, they didn't send the police. After all,
what if those present were better armed? No, for clashes with
the underworld of gambling and organized crime, they sent
the army.

Everyone scurried away in different directions like cock-
roaches. The boy opened the driver-side door of a Volk-
swagen bug. Sitting on a pillow to see over the steering wheel,
he dug around in his pants pocket and pulled out a key. The
passenger door opened, and a man sat down.

"Let's go, Santiago."

"Yes, Dad." And the boy straightened his leg to press the
accelerator.

THIS IS THE STORY OF A FATHER, A SON, AND THE TWO different men each would each become.

Years earlier, this father never went to clandestine cock-fights, much less his little boy Santiago. But the glow of gold can seduce a man, hypnotize him so he does things he never thought of doing, so he goes places he never imagined he'd go. Let's go back to a time when this family believed nights were for sleeping and days for working honestly.

The man lived in a small town bordered by the Sierra Madre Occidental of Mexico. Arteaga, barely a point on the map, was a little town with one gasoline station and only one roundabout. Like many government-employed teachers, the man worked wherever they sent him, and they tended to send people to the farthest-flung villages of the country, like Arteaga.

In Arteaga, he had all the fresh coconuts he could ever want, but that didn't compensate for what this teacher had left behind. In a blink of an eye, he would have traded the warm Pacific breeze and the mountain views of Arteaga to have his family close by. His wife and children were living many long hours inland in the city of Morelia.

In this way, the man's life was torn in two.

With every paycheck he received, he would send money to support his wife, and every month, he drove those serpentine highways back home. When he couldn't be with his loved ones, their voices on the telephone helped him hold out.

Like many young couples, they made ends meet. His wife, in addition to being a teacher herself, was a bargain hunter. Although they never went hungry, they found that if you always have to tighten your belt, you're never comfortable.

It was at this time when the man stumbled upon treasure. It wasn't stacks of Spanish doubloons or a briefcase full of cash, but it was close: an unexpected pay raise. From one day to the next, the man's salary quadrupled. For the first time in his life, he had to think: *Now what do I do with all this income?*

Remodel their house in Morelia? Buy new clothes for his kids? Surprise his wife with a trip to Hawaii? Yes, yes, yes, it all sounded good. Of course he would do it. He would do it all— and more! But first, he wanted to feel rich, if only for a moment in his life.

When he cashed his copious paycheck, he sent home the same amount as always.

That day, the teacher went right on by the open-air market and went straight to a new territory: the mall. In one store, the man sat down with a cardboard box in his hands. When he opened the lid, light seemed to emanate from within. Thin paper covered the contents of the box. *A gift*, he thought, *a gift to myself.* He smiled and took out a pair of sneakers. The stitches, the leather, the soles… everything was designed to German perfection.

This wasn't anything like buying shoes in the market. There among all the other articles of used clothing on a tarp on the ground, he used to buy whatever he'd find in his size. If by chance he liked the style, that was icing on the cake.

But today, the man would buy exactly what he wished. On his feet, his new shoes gripped his heel and adjusted themselves to his arches like destiny itself. He stopped in front of a full-length mirror. He saw that logo on his feet— the logo that for all his youth had been just for the rich, cool people. Could it be that today he would become one of them?

This thought was interrupted by another: with the amount of money listed on the shoes' price tag, he could feed his family for three weeks. He took off the shoes and returned them to the box. "They *will* eat well," he promised himself, "and dress like kings too. But it's my turn first." He left the store with a swagger in his steps. It wasn't just the shoes that were new; he felt like a brand-new man.

On his way home, a new thought occurred to him: *Instead of always having rice and beans, why not go to a restaurant every once in a while?* There wasn't a reason to suffer anymore. Following the same logic, his pantry filled bottle by bottle with liquor.

Payday after payday, like a post-surgery patient who gets addicted to morphine, the man acquired a taste for his double life. Everything was new: shirts, belt buckles, glasses, suit jackets. He vowed he would take his wife and kids to all the nicest stores and fill out their wardrobes too. Just not yet.

One night, he went to a dance club. To his surprise, he locked eyes with a couple of girls half his age. He let his eyes wander over their curves. With a few drinks in him, he went over and flirted. He hadn't felt like a "conquistador" in years.

Perhaps it was that night, or maybe it happened on one of the many nights that followed, but the man stopped remembering his promise. He had pushed it to the horizon so many times, it had fallen off the edge of the earth. He was living a double life and hadn't expected it to feel so good.

One interest became his obsession: cockfights.

It seemed like nothing was going to stop the man's ongoing fiesta until a bus rolled into Arteaga one day. And who got off it but the man's son, Santiago? How he'd managed to convince his mother to let him go, the man didn't know. The boy dropped his suitcase and ran over to hug his dad. The man's smile barely masked what he was thinking: this reunion felt more like an intrusion.

How could he carry on his lifestyle in front of his thirteen-year-old son? He analyzed the problem from every angle as if it were a Rubik's cube. His extra income, his late-night outings, everything had to stay a secret. But one thing was keeping his lifestyle *secret*, and another was *abolishing* it altogether.

Would he quit all the things he liked cold turkey just so that Santiago wouldn't find out about them? If he did, what would he do with all his money? No, that was no good. Well, what he was doing had to stay a secret. But a secret from who?

Suddenly, all the colors of the cube fell into place; he had solved it: as long as his wife didn't find out, everything would be fine.

Silence came at the price of the child's impulses. Soon Santi owned the latest electronic gadgets and dressed dapper like his dad. He picked up the salty lingo of his dad's party friends and spoke with no fear of punishment. With each little bribe, Dad's secret became "our secret."

The coming of Santiago turned out to be far more beneficial than the man could have dreamed. When there was a faraway cockfight and he had to work the next day, now he had a road companion. With a few driving lessons for Santi, the man could lean back in the passenger seat and take a nap.

There was another advantage too. Communication with his wife had gotten uncomfortable. If the man needed to say something to her, Santiago was their little messenger.

With the situation set up this perfectly, what could go wrong?

"SON, WAKE UP. I NEED YOU TO TAKE ME SOMEWHERE." Santiago, already asleep in bed, moaned in protest. It was eleven at night, but his dad wanted to gamble at a cockfight. As per usual, Santiago was going to drive the truck, and his dad would sleep on the way.

Now sixteen years old, Santiago had experience "tearing around the curves," as his mother had said indignantly. She'd found out about some things, and she didn't like it that her son was behind the wheel on the mountain highways, one misstep from plummeting down a canyon. His father, for his part, gave Santiago a tip: "It's just you and me out there, so... keep watch."

Generally, it's the kids who place their destinies in their

parents' hands, but in this case, all of the responsibility fell upon a sleepy teenager. His dad reclined his seat to rest, and after fifteen minutes, he was snoring. A few minutes more down the road, and Santi gave in as well.

Santiago opened his eyes and saw they were veering off the highway. No turn of the wheel and no braking would stop their impact with the forest. Today, Santiago affirms God helped him to react in that instant: he lifted his legs and laid on his father's lap. With a deafening noise, the car rolled, launching bits of glass throughout the cabin of the truck. Tree branches clawed it up, shredding the metal and rubber. The steering wheel extended outward and upward as if the steering column had been a javelin. It perforated the roof of the truck. The front wheel burst up through the driver-side floor.

After a few seconds, the commotion stopped. The passengers stayed in their seats, still breathing. Santiago got out through the gash that used to be his door. The two checked themselves in the light of the still-gleaming headlights. Santiago's hand was fractured, his shins had deep contusions, and his face was bloody from a cut in his eyebrow. His father looked himself over: not a scratch.

In silence, they walked down the road and took a taxi to the hospital. They sold the remains of the truck for scrap metal. The man would have sold the memory of that night too if he could have, because he never asked Santiago how he was or what had happened. From the night of the accident until this day, they never talked about it.

Santiago had to reflect: his father wouldn't let go of his sins or the benefits that went with them. Doing that had left his marriage disfigured. Betrayal, lies, and distrust filled the places where love should have been. His absence had left his children without the identity a father gives. And his inheritance for them? He had squandered it all.

A YEAR AFTER THE ACCIDENT, SANTIAGO EXPERIENCED AN impact of another kind. His aunt had paid for him to go to summer camp. As a scout who already knew about knots and nature, he said yes to the offer without thinking twice.

As he'd expected, they played team games, yelled, and ran around in juvenile chaos. But what took him by surprise was hearing the message of Jesus Christ in a meeting. Even at Santiago's age of seventeen years old, he'd never heard anyone ever speak about Him, not even to say "God loves you."

Santiago paid attention. He thought, *Wait a minute, did someone tell the preacher about me?* Because everything the preacher said seemed like it was just for Santiago. The young man felt so moved that he couldn't hold back his tears.

This was what had been missing in his life. Jesus describes the discovery like this:

> The kingdom of heaven is like treasure hidden in a field, which a man found and covered up. Then in his joy he goes and sells all that he has and buys that field. (Matthew 13:44)

The first thing the man in the parable did was *see*. He had to see the field and recognize it wasn't just a place to grow corn or play soccer, but there was treasure buried there. Maybe he had passed by that place a hundred times before and not seen it. Maybe you've gone to church services a hundred times before, but have you truly *seen*?

The next thing the man did was sell everything he had. As far as Santiago was concerned, he would exchange all his vices for the kingdom of heaven.

He started by quitting the cockfights. His dad continued to invite him, but Santiago gave him a whole spectrum of excuses. He even said one time he couldn't go because he had a lot of homework. *Homework? Seriously?* His dad didn't believe it. Santiago was the laziest kid ever. If he made excuses, it was to *get out of* his studies. (By the way, he eventually graduated from high school and later earned his undergraduate degree in industrial engineering.)

Santiago also stopped dating multiple girls at the same time. He renounced the excitement of the chase and the pleasure of one-night stands. Along with this, he stopped smoking and drinking alcohol, which had become occasions for losing control.

Supernaturally, from one day to the next, he didn't feel like doing any of those things. He described it like taking off dirty clothes, like when you peel your soaking-wet socks off your feet to step into a hot shower—that drastic.

In the verse, "In his joy he goes and sells all that he has," did you notice the phrase "in his joy"? When Santiago talks about his past, it's only at this point in the story that he gets happy. His voice jumps an octave, and his face illuminates.

By contrast, his father thought about all his son was losing. To him, the gospel was just a bunch of words, Jesus was just a guy, and the field was just a field. He couldn't see the treasure below the surface. Not everyone will see it.

The last part of the parable is this: "...and buys that field." You receive something. It's not about renouncing and renouncing. If you love God, what you receive is the key to the kingdom of heaven.

You may have occasionally wondered what the kingdom of heaven is; I have too. This definition has served me well: it's the people of God in the place of God under His rule and reign.[1] An inheritance such as the kingdom deserves a whole book unto itself to explore the dimensions of these three things. But we can dedicate a few paragraphs here to examine one of its benefits: the people of God.

They weren't anything like the people he'd met in crazy parties getting smashed. The only thing that brought the partygoers together was alcohol. Booze gets sticky when it dries, but it isn't a strong adhesive and certainly not one strong enough to hold lives together.

With the followers of Jesus that Santiago met, it was different. He saw firsthand how people ought to treat *one another.*

> Live in harmony with **one another**. Do not be haughty, but associate with the lowly. Never be wise in your own sight. (Romans 12:16 emphasis mine in this and the following verses)
>
> Be kind to **one another**, tenderhearted, forgiving **one another**, as God in Christ forgave you. (Ephesians 4:32)
>
> Do not speak evil against **one another**, brothers. The one who speaks against a brother or judges his brother, speaks evil against the law and judges the law. But if you judge the law, you are not a doer of the law but a judge. (James 4:11)
>
> Therefore, confess your sins to **one another** and pray for **one another**, that you may be healed. The prayer of a righteous person has great power as it is working. (James 5:16)

Is this not over-the-top good? There are ninety-four verses in the Bible that refer to "one another." If you have a community with this kind of love written into its DNA, you are rich. Literally. Economists call it "social capital."

Speaking of economists, at his church Más Vida, Santiago met Dr. Andrés Panasiuk. This pastor was about to launch a ministry that teaches personal finance, and he needed an assistant. Santiago offered himself. As they worked together, Santiago absorbed as much learning as he could.

Dr. Panasiuk has many titles: conference speaker, bestselling author, pastor, professor, and founder of Cultura Financiera. In those days, he added one more: spiritual father.

He guided Santiago through his formative years in the faith, helping him take his first steps of maturity.

Out of all the people enriching Santiago's life, he couldn't keep his eyes off one. Her complexion was of sweet cream complexion and her features were obsidian dark. She smiled with her eyes. Dinora was a woman who, like him, was beloved and redeemed by God. Her adolescence as a gang member is a story for another day, but suffice it to say, she is a live wire. How could they not fall in love? Surrounded by friends, mentors, children, pastors, and family—the people of God—Dinora and Santiago made their lifelong vows and became man and wife.

These people are beautiful though imperfect reflections of their Creator. He is the King, and Santiago knew he would give anything to be a part of that kingdom.

FRIEND, PAY CLOSE ATTENTION TO THE OBJECT OF YOUR DESIRE. There is room in your heart for only one treasure. Be careful because, in the end, it will be yours.

SIXTEEN
HONOR
A HEAVIER TOPIC

"Stop right now!" The girl shouted between gasps. She pedaled her bike violently, crunching the gravel beneath her wheels. With her eyes narrowed and teeth clenched, she looked like a fighter pilot.

Just meters in front of her, a boy was running his heart out, a strap from his overalls loose and bouncing with his steps. The two of them continued in a frenzy that this residential street normally didn't see.

The country had just gone through the Great Depression: unemployed men, thousands of people in lines for bread provided by the government, families thrown out of their apartments. I've seen black-and-white pictures from that time, and in none of them are people smiling.

That's why if you had a bicycle, you *had* something. If it was a Schwinn, forget about it. That beauty looked like it came from the future, what with its electric headlamp and spring seat. Even the frame looked like the fuselage of an airplane.

The girl's bike was so special that ten minutes ago, the boy in the overalls gave a mischievous grin and said, "That's a beautiful bike right there. It would sure be a *shame* if anything happened to it."

The message was clear, but the girl wasn't going to be intimidated by this little extortioner. Oh no, it was he who would pay, and so the chase began.

"Come back here, you coward!" yelled the furious schoolgirl.

The boy looked over his shoulder, eyes wide. His newsie cap fell to the ground and quickly got run over.

He made his way to the enormous porch of a house. "Open up!" he screamed as he crossed the front yard. His mom looked out through the window.

The girl kept coming. If he made it inside to the refuge of his house, would he get away with it? Would she have to put up with him and his bully friends tomorrow in the schoolyard? She threw the bike to the grass and began to run.

With his heart beating in his ears, the boy ran up the stairs to the front door and went inside. Finally feeling safe in his living room, he grabbed the knob to close the door. Before he could hear the click of the lock, though, the door exploded open on its hinges.

There in the backlight of the open doorframe was the silhouette of the girl, her curly hair bouncing as she panted. This young vigilante was my grandmother Lorraine.

She leaped on the boy and bowled him over. The two rolled around on the living room carpet and knocked over the lamp.

"Lorraine, okay, I'm sorry!"

"You're GONNA be sorry!"

The boy's mother covered her mouth with both hands as she saw Lorraine, now sitting on the boy's chest, drop the knockout punch.

You might say I have a savage lineage.

YEARS WENT BY AND WITH THEM THE WAR OF THE '40s. Lorraine grew up to be a young lady in the '50s. In those days, Americans wanted to settle down: they bought homes and had a lot of kids. Lorraine married my grandfather Harvey.

If you have ever seen movies from that period, you'll know it was a time of pure family bliss. At the head of the table sat the father with his jacket and tie. A gentleman, he directed the conversation. The well-groomed kids talked about their day's adventures, and every once in a while, their mother interjected with wise comments from the other end of the table. She was a serene presence in the home.

My father's childhood had some things in common with these. They went on summer camping trips to the beach, for instance. Lorraine was an outstanding baker, and her chocolate cake was extraordinary. Harvey was a resourceful man who knew how to work with his hands. And my dad and his brothers roved and explored like Tom Sawyer.

But many aspects of his early years were quite unlike the old movies. The words "serene" and "wise" didn't fit my grandmother very well. She was pure dynamite. The benefit was that no one messed with the family; there were no tyrant teachers or bullies from the neighborhood. She knew how to defend her own. But the thing about dynamite is you don't want to be close when it goes off.

And it went off at unexpected times. They could be relaxing at home on a summer day or celebrating a birthday with my grandma's chocolate cake, and out of nowhere, some "provocation"—maybe a pair of shoes not put away in the right place—would awaken my grandmother's wrath. Any happiness in that moment would abruptly come to an end.

Of course, it wasn't the shoes that provoked her. Her kids didn't know the adult pressures she was dealing with. Money was always tight in those days, and my grandfather did more than his part to set her off.

Whatever the inner workings of his family dynamic might

have been, my dad couldn't lower his defenses and be at ease when he was at home.

He told me that many nights in his bed, his face under the covers, he would cry. How could he sleep? His bedroom shuddered from the explosive arguments of my grandparents in the kitchen on the other side of the wall. My grandma's words flew at the top of her voice like shrapnel. Lorraine even threw plates to the floor if her point wasn't clear enough.

Today, my father's house is still standing in the neighborhood where he grew up. But at some point, the Moses home collapsed under the bombardment. Everything ended in divorce, and the kids eventually moved from Massachusetts to other states.

I WAS BORN IN THE PACIFIC NORTHWEST, THREE THOUSAND miles and three time zones away from Massachusetts. Although we visited in the summers, I knew my grandmother mainly through phone calls. We would pass the receiver to one another, stretching the spiral cable. She told us about her work as a school bus driver. I told her about the plays I made as the catcher on my baseball team.

Distance can be a good thing. Problems happen when you're close to someone, but distance keeps you out of the blast radius. I think my dad had enough emotional rubble from his past. He didn't need any more in the present.

JESUS OFTEN QUOTED THE OLD TESTAMENT WHEN HE preached. I like that. In doing so, He was saying that what was true back then is still true today—in other words, that this is how life has always worked.

One ancient command He quoted was "Honor your father and your mother." Lorraine has made me think about

this phrase a lot recently. I had trouble formulating a definition of the word *honor*, maybe because I speak so informally or
because I like rap music. What occurred to me first was a
samurai bowing before his emperor. So I looked it up in a
dictionary—a biblical Greek dictionary because I wondered
what Jesus meant when He said it.

It means *heavy*. That's strange. What does *heavy* have to do
with *honor*?

I guess if you throw a heavy stone into a lake, it splashes
out concentric waves. Honorable people have this way of
affecting everyone around them. Their eye contact lets you
know you're heard. Their words, chosen not chucked, say so
much.

I thought about another similarity. Sometimes when I
compare products, I hold both of them to feel their weight.
You can feel the difference between plastic and steel, between
the cheap stuff and the good stuff. It's like that with honorable
people too. They're so excellent, you can feel the weight of
their presence—their gravitas. It seems like everything they
touch is heavy too. You don't think twice about buying their
book, going to their event, or taking their advice.

The opposite of *heavy* is *light*. Some people aren't worth
your time. Haven't you ever swiped quickly over certain
people's Instagram stories? Their pictures and words are as
flimsy as leaves; far from penetrating your heart, they bounce
off your forehead and float to the ground. You could say that
is *not* honor.

The question is, how do you honor a parent who
hurt you?

ONE DAY, THIS QUESTION STOPPED BEING THEORETICAL.
Lorraine had fallen during a snowstorm and was in the hospital. There they discovered she had dementia. The only way
forward was for her to move to Oregon, closer to family.

This meant numerous weeks of hard work for my parents, aunts, and uncles. They would have to take various coast-to-coast flights. They would have to pack up or sell my grandma's mountainous accumulation of possessions. On top of that, an assisted living home equipped to properly care for her would cost a fortune.

When you are just about to help someone, have you ever asked yourself this question: *But what have they done for me?* When the other kids in his middle school were on the baseball diamond, my dad was working as a janitor in his family's business. When my dad wanted to get somewhere, his parents didn't take him; he had to walk or hitchhike. He sometimes ate nothing but crackers for dinner because they had no other food in the house. When he wanted to go to college, he paid for it himself. Helping a person who neglected you. The irony hit a nerve.

If that weren't enough, another fight was about to break out. Like many elderly people who have feared losing their independence, my grandmother demanded to stay in her house. In spite of everything the doctors said, she thought her health would get better. What's more, she argued, why should she go? She'd lived in Massachusetts her whole life. No, no, and no. Everyone should just stop bothering her, and *no one* was going to sell any of her things.

Well then.

If she wanted to handle this by herself so badly...

Would my dad wash his hands of this? Although it sounded tempting, he couldn't do that. My grandmother wanted independence but needed honor.

It took weeks of begging and arguments, but finally, Lorraine gave in and moved to Oregon. There, our life took a new shape. We learned to fold up the wheelchair and put it in the trunk. We learned her medicine schedule. Our routine adjusted itself to the visits we made to the care home where she lived. I'll tell you, we're now pretty good at bingo and arts and crafts. Here was a nice surprise: we became friends with the caretakers of the home, a friendly Romanian couple.

My dad still took care of his mother even when he wasn't at the care home. In his office, he studied line after line of financial documents and made phone calls to therapists. Several times, he had to drive her to the hospital.

Even with her dementia, Lorraine's personality remained prickly, more of a porcupine than a puppy. One time, she fought with another granny. It wasn't a spectacle like one from her robust years, but she did manage to whack the lady with a spoon. Later, when she and my mom went shopping, Lorraine was quite the fighter pilot in a scooter. She zoomed down the grocery store aisles, leaving my mom in her dust!

But oh how my grandma melted when my dad gave her little shoulder massages. She would close her eyes and sometimes purr. My dad used to finish each massage by giving her a kiss on the forehead.

JESUS TOLD US TO HONOR OUR PARENTS. THERE ARE NO conditional clauses, such as if they have dementia or if you didn't have a happy childhood. Just give them honor. Let their words have weight. Let their presence have importance. Let them be valuable in your eyes.

Jesus didn't give us an out from this command, but He did add a promise: "'Honor your father and mother'—which is the first command with a promise—'so that it may go well with you and that you may enjoy long life on the earth'" (Ephesians 6:2–3 NIV).

I saw the fulfillment of this promise one year at Christmas. In the living room of the home where my grandma lived stood an enormous fir tree trimmed with lights and ornaments. The fireplace was crackling. The aroma of turkey and cinnamon saturated the air. I was sitting on the sofa with my guitar in my lap when my dad brought my grandmother out of her room in her wheelchair. She looked good: nails painted, hair done, and Christmas sweater on. She looked up at my dad, and the two of them smiled at each other while we all sang carols.

What happened inside my father was even more beautiful; the wounds that time had not healed finally stopped bleeding. My dad told me later he finally felt peace with his mother. It wasn't because she said, "I love you" or "Forgive me," although that would have meant a lot. The peace he experienced was a gift from God, and He gave it to my father by simple means:

Honor.

SEVENTEEN
POWER AND AUTHORITY
HOW CENTRO NOE WAS FOUNDED

But Jesus called them together and said, "You know that the rulers in this world lord it over their people, and officials flaunt their authority over those under them."
Matthew 20:25 NLT

Jesus said this in Roman times. Although the Romans produced many good things, like highways and aqueducts, they also inflicted incalculable harm. Their economy depended on slaves. They mobilized their armies to massacre and conquer nations. Their empire was the very definition of the abuse of power.

It's been like that since just about the beginning. In Genesis, there was a man named Lamech—a descendent of Cain, the first murderer. Lamech was proud of his ancestor's bad-boy reputation. He wrote a song in which he boasted about having not one but two wives. And he didn't kill one person, but two. Imagine that: Lamech was the first *machista* with the first gangsta rap song ever.

If you turn the pages of textbooks, you'll see tyranny

throughout human history. The only thing that changes is which nation dominates the rest.

So, what should we do?

Rise up and fight, right? Overthrow the dictator, drive out the invaders, beat the other party, all that? This is called a power struggle. If other people are going to oppress us with their authority, we have to take it away from them.

Power struggles happen even here in my beautiful Mexico. Among the ancient pyramids and Caribbean lagoons and the vast deserts and towering mountains of this country, there is strife.

I see it especially in my field of work: education. Every year, the main avenues fill with people marching. Usually, they're teachers demanding the salaries they had been promised but never received. The college students training to be teachers prefer to put up a fight in more colorful ways: they regularly act like pirates to recuperate funds they believe they are entitled to. They take over tollbooths and charge motorists their own toll. They even hijack buses to extort money out of local businesses.

In an ironic twist, the same teachers who see themselves as victims of their superiors are seen as despots by their pupils. By force, these outraged students commonly occupy entire buildings on university campuses for weeks until their demands are met.

Mexico's federal government passed a national education reform to curb embezzlement. Since many teachers' unions saw their income affected, they resisted the law.

Unfortunately, almost nothing gets solved in power struggles. Even when one group wins, they normally become the next oppressors.

In the midst of all this discord, don't you want to know what Jesus said about it? Let's go back to the verse that opened the chapter and read on. "You know that the rulers in this world lord it over their people, and officials flaunt their authority over those under them. But among you it will be different. Whoever wants to be a leader among you must be your servant, and whoever wants to be first among you must become your slave. '" (Matthew 20:25–27 NLT).

Now I will tell you the story of a woman and her friends who decided to become servants.

In 1980, Laurie Henkle had never seen a small-town plaza at sunset. She didn't know corn could be prepared with a stick, cream, cheese, and chile. She couldn't pronounce the Spanish "R." In the hazelnut eyes of this American girl, all of Mexico seemed new.

She was traveling with Elsa, her friend from high school. Exploring Mexico is worth doing just for its own sake, but Laurie was there for more than that. These girls went to Sonora because Laurie wanted to visit Elsa's stomping grounds and meet her family.

One day during their stay, Laurie saw something else she hadn't seen before: barefoot children selling candy at a highway intersection. They were eight-year-old kids who should have been reading and painting in elementary school, but here they were, dodging traffic.

If Laurie had shrugged her shoulders and walked on, it would have been understandable. She was only a tourist. But she stood there thinking, her dark brown hair fluttering in the desert wind. Elsa noticed her friend's concern, so she explained that the teachers were once again on strike, and sometimes students lost months of classes. To get some benefit out of their idle days, kids went out to work.

How can that be? thought Laurie. It wasn't that she had any aversion to work. After all, she'd had a newspaper route in elementary school. She knew if work experience is enriched by mathematics and books, it can be an upward trajectory toward success. Jobs can be a laboratory where young people experiment with what they've learned, but this—selling candies to passing cars—was not that.

Another thing about the kids made her uneasy. In the afternoons when Laurie wasn't at school, she spent her time on a basketball court in the safety of a community center. Unlike herself, these kids were outside on the street for most of the day, exposed to the elements, to knives, and to any kind of creep on the prowl.

What were these little angels actually selling—candy or their futures?

By 1990, LAURIE WASN'T A SCHOOLGIRL ANYMORE. MAYBE you wouldn't have guessed it by looking at this lovely young woman, but she owned a brand of athletic clothing that sold nationwide. In college, Laurie had experienced success selling T-shirts with her screen printing machine, so she turned it into a small business out of her mom's garage. With hard work, the business grew and grew.

Those who speak Spanish can see Laurie's heart in the name she chose for her company: Brindar Design. In Spanish, *brindar* means "to provide." From the very start, she wanted the profit from her business to provide help for kids like those she'd seen on the highway.

I think this is the humble path of service Jesus was talking about. Laurie decided to take it, and it led her once again to Mexico with Elsa.

Together they crossed the northern deserts of Mexico, their bus just a black speck on the horizon beneath the vast blue sky. They navigated in taxis through Mexican cities, mazes of open-air markets, colonial palaces, and modern towers. They arrived at charity organizations, which they interviewed. They wanted to know what young people in Mexico needed and how Brindar could help them effectively.

. . .

Solidifying a vision was going to take time, but Laurie soon learned that sending monetary donations was not a good strategy. It would be better to spend Brindar's funds on people's salaries. People, not dollar bills, would make a difference. All she needed to do was find them!

So Laurie shared her dream with those closest to her: her friends. Elsa wanted to back it, of course. The artist who illustrated a popular design for the business, Margaret, loved the cause. Her husband Brett joined without thinking twice. He was a pastor with a heart for young people. He knew some new people in their church, Brian and Mireya. They were a young married couple getting settled in the city, and they offered to support in any way they could.

Here they were: Team Brindar. They didn't know how they were going to do it, but they wanted to help the kids.

If your goal is to serve, you should know that being a slave is not glamorous. Brindar decided to humble Brett and Margaret the quickest way possible: make them learn a new language.

So they went to Mexico City to start learning. They discovered the Spaniards didn't leave any word all by itself. They added an ending to each one! In English, it's enough to just stick an "S" on the end of a word sometimes, like the way *"eat"* becomes *"eats,"* but in Spanish, the same word can become *"como," "comes," "come," "comemos," "coméis," and "comen."*

The theory Brett and Margaret learned gave them a basis for the language, but they wanted to continue their education outside the classroom. So they lived with a Mexican family for a few weeks. This family had a father, a mother, and a daughter named Cuca. Brett and Margaret rented a room and pitched in so they could have breakfast with the family every day.

When you are a beginner sitting at the table with native speakers, you can barely piece together the words being said to you. Take this example conversation:

MOTHER: *Brett,* ¿ฉันจะเสิร์ฟเค้กอร่อย ๆ ให้คุณได้ไหม *chilaquiles?*

Judging by the plates in front of you, you know more or less what she is talking about. But it's a strong dose of humility when you realize that even kids, in this case, Cuca, can speak better than you.

CUCA: ผมชอบสีแดง ¿คุณชอบสีเขียวหรือไม่, *Margaret?*

How do you respond to that? I'll give you a tip: smile and nod your head. Little by little, you'll learn to communicate with all these people you love. Just take it one breakfast at a time.

BRETT: *Chilaquiles. (Points to the empty plate) Muy rica. Mucho gracias. (Puts two thumbs up)*

ONE OF THE INTERVIEWS THAT BRINDAR CONDUCTED WAS with Dr. Rafael Díaz, the regional director of the government family service called Desarrollo Integral de la Familia. He was a good person to know because they helped families in extreme conditions. Since Laurie wasn't there, it fell on Brett to do the interview. His Spanish would have to rise to the occasion when he spoke with this important man.

In Dr. Díaz's office, it turned out that Brett had to speak more than anyone. The doctor asked him question after question, an interview in reverse, and Brett fumbled with his words to answer them. Brett helped Dr. Díaz understand Brindar's concern for children, above all those who are vulnerable.

At the end of two hours, Brett was red-faced and sweating from his lexical efforts.

Dr. Díaz then said, "Very well. I love the vision and what you want to do."

Brett's jaw dropped. Dr. Díaz had known English the whole time! They shared a laugh, and the doctor told him he had studied his specialization in the United States. When the meeting was over, Dr. Díaz insisted Brindar bring their vision to Morelia, the capital of the state of Michoacán.

When you have a mission, sometimes you run, sometimes you jog, and then there are the times when you have no other choice but to take a leap. If you know where the project is going to be, what is your next step?

Go.

In the summer of 1991, Laurie, Elsa, Brett, Margaret, Brian, and Mireya left behind houses, jobs, cars, and parents. They moved to Morelia. What remained to research and figure out, they would do there.

Once they'd moved in, Brian and Mireya's apartment turned into their war room, but instead of Winston Churchill with a map of Europe, there were six twenty-somethings with a map of Morelia. There they wrote down notes and filled up chalkboards. They set goals like meeting with pastors from local churches and looking for a building for their operation. They debated ideas like starting a private school or an orphanage. They always prayed to God, committing their plans to Him.

An idea crystallized in the war room. It was called New Opportunities in Education, or for short, the NOE Center. It would be a place that stood in the gap for youth: homework help to make up for what they were missing in school, English tutoring so they could get better jobs, and music and art lessons too. If the schools were closed, NOE would have its doors open. And these teachers would integrate Christ's love and His teachings into each class.

Because of Brindar's financial support, they would be able to charge low tuition within everyone's reach, even the families of kids who sold candy at intersections.

One of the first tasks was to find a building. Morelia is a city of grandiose buildings. They have limestone facades so tall they block out the sun. You arch your neck to see the balconies where princesses once upon a time came out to see their suitors.

Inside, the ceilings soar eighteen feet high. You feel the need to stand up straight like one of the pillars in the inner courtyard. You're no viceroy or archbishop, but with good posture, hopefully they won't kick you out.

In October, the NOE Center team found a building like this in downtown Morelia. It was big, institutional, and respectable. They paid the security deposit and the first month's rent. The next day, they planned how they would set up the classrooms. That same day, the owner of the building came out to greet them. He gave them back the envelope with the payment they had given him. Looking at the ground and shaking his head, he told them he couldn't rent them the building. His Catholic priest had warned him to have nothing to do with the NOE Center because they would be teaching Bible verses.

After the initial shock, the team got together again to pray. They knew God had a plan and would provide. What if that "no" had been a "yes" for something better?

They found another building. Rather, it was a house in a

working-class neighborhood. One of the requirements of the rental contract was a cosigner of good repute. The owner of the house was surprised when he saw NOE's cosigner was Dr. Rafael Díaz!

After signing and getting NOE going, they discovered how cozy the space felt. Students sat in the sofas after class and chatted, or played Ping-Pong in the garage. A few of them considered NOE their home away from home. The schools downtown didn't have that effect. I guess that's because only the humble make you feel like you belong.

Months passed by, and the rainy season began. Brian walked past the other building, the one they hadn't been able to rent. He stopped for a moment to see that the whole block was flooded under three feet of water. A car was floating out front!

"WE WERE JUST KIDS WITHOUT MUCH EXPERIENCE OR MANY accomplishments in life," remembers Brett. Maybe you are young too. The good thing about serving others is that it's about what you give, not about what you have or what you've already done in life.

Brett and Brian didn't have much, but these gringos were good at jumping. As they walked around the neighborhood, they went by an athletic complex. They heard a familiar pounding sound. They glanced inside to see people dribbling basketballs. Brian and Brett looked at each other with smiles. They went into the complex to play, and between passes and baskets, they got to know the guys.

In no time, a group of teens took the court in blue uniforms, the Cougars of the NOE Center. Now Brian and Brett could invest in their students' lives outside the classroom. As coaches, they showed their students how to improve—not by shortcuts, but through simple discipline.

ONCE THE PROGRAM HAD BEEN RUNNING FOR A FEW YEARS, IT became clear the center needed accreditation for its alumni. A nationally recognized diploma would help the students get jobs.

But that meant NOE would have to be registered with the Secretary of Public Education, the epicenter of the educational power struggle in the country. Dealing with the Secretary would be a sticky tangle of bureaucracy. It could take years. It could cost a fortune. Like Jesus said: "You know that the rulers in this world lord it over their people, and officials flaunt their authority over those under them." Teeth clenched, they went to the Secretary of Public Education's office.

When they entered, who greeted them from her desk but Cuca from Brett and Margaret's host family! She made the work to get accredited much easier and faster than it could have been. From that day forward, every alumnus of NOE has received an official, nationally recognized diploma.

JESUS GAVE A PARADOX TO US: THE LOWER YOU GET DOWN TO serve others, the greater you become. It may not seem true at first, but you can see it with your own eyes: today NOE has been working for more than twenty-five years, and it has opened four campuses in Morelia, Michoacán, and León, Guanajuato. More than a thousand people come through their doors each week to participate in their programs. And there are results! Eighty-six percent of NOE's students graduate high school. That's five times more than the state average.[1] The English they learn helps them earn thirty to fifty percent higher salaries at work.[2] NOE graduates today are teachers, dentists, accountants, engineers, architects, pastors, and doctors.

You know you are in the presence of greatness when you see Mariela's smile. When this girl came to NOE, she was devastated by circumstances in her family. She was a bomb that could go off in tears at any moment. I don't know everything that happened in her life to make her smile these days, but I know her favorite shoes were a gift from Director Hugo. I know that teachers greet her by name while she skips down the hall to her reading class. I know she and her grandmother decided to put their faith in Christ in NOE's office.

Power and authority exist for the good of the people in your care. I think that's why NOE's teachers are never on strike. From the day it was founded until now, they have never missed a paycheck.

I can't fit into one chapter the stories of Director Juan, who puts on his cleats and takes the boys from the orphanage to indoor soccer after classes, or the Americans who have visited and fallen in love with NOE students, or the twenty-three Dream Teams that NOE has sent to the USA for summer cultural exchanges, or the friendships between students that last well after their courses end, or the entire families that have come to know Christ through their sons and daughters who attend the Bible studies. In the eyes of God, this is true greatness.

JESUS SAID THAT THE GOVERNORS OF THIS WORLD EXERCISE authority over their subjects. He didn't say "some do it" or "only certain countries do it." He said this as a simple fact of life: this is how people are, all of them. You can see that arrogance on the sports fields; you can see that misuse of power among coworkers; you can see tiny despots even on the school playground.

Jesus was talking about the human condition. We are sinful, and He was describing how sinful people use power. If there is ever hope for the restoration of the halls of power, we need liberation from sin.

This brings us to our final verse in the passage. "Whoever

wants to be a leader among you must be your servant, and whoever wants to be first among you must become your slave. *For even the Son of Man came not to be served but to serve others and to give his life as a ransom for many.*" (Matthew 20:26–28 NLT emphasis mine).

Jesus Christ used His power to rescue us from the corruption of our hearts. Since He, the King of Creation, treated us with humility, you and I can exercise our authority in service of others. We can leave the strutting and posturing behind because, like Laurie and her friends, we're going after true greatness.

EIGHTEEN

WHO YOU TURN TO

ALEX AND THE DIAGNOSIS

It was midnight when I got Alex's message. In those late hours, I seldom respond to anyone; they're booked up for sleeping. But it's different with Alex. We have an evergreen friendship with long roots. Few people in the world know me like Alex does. Now that I live in Mexico, his text messages get me excited.

But that night when I touched the screen and read his words, I couldn't stay flat on my bed. I sat up as what he had written registered in my head. It was the longest message he had ever sent me, and he was asking for prayer. They had diagnosed him with ankylosing spondylitis.

If you've never heard of ankylosing spondylitis (AS), let me explain. It's a kind of arthritis in the spine and pelvis. Doctors don't understand this pathology completely, but they say it's genetic. It's the tragedy of friendly fire: the autoimmune system, which is supposed to defend the body from viruses and harmful bacteria, actually attacks its own joints. These parts of the body, which are designed to move freely, seize up. In the worst cases, they fuse together and stop pivoting. And so the life of AS patients becomes mitigation of chronic pain and trying to slow the breakdown of the body.

I would never have predicted that Alex would stop moving. He is one of the few people I know who doesn't settle for running marathons. He completed a race that was fifty kilometers through mountain trails. He didn't drive his car downtown to work like any other nine-to-fiver; he cycled those fourteen miles with spandex and everything. While some like to "Netflix and chill," he preferred to rock gym and thrill. Alex was the archetype of a body in motion.

There's one more symptom of AS worth mentioning. I'm not a biologist to be able to understand what this has to do with spinal arthritis, but many patients with AS experience deterioration in their vision. Alex found this out when he visited the doctor. He went in because his vision was blurry. So on top of everything, he would become blind?

Sitting on my bed, I cried with my phone in my hands.

Have you ever seen antique maps? They are works of art: precise lines and calligraphy on parchment. I've wondered what kind of person became a cartographer to calculate the distances and the topography in those days. If Alex had been born in another century, I think he might have been one. He's always known where he's wanted to go, and he traces routes to get there. He has a chalkboard in his room where he writes his short-term and long-term goals. In the years I lived with him, I watched as, one by one, he completed them.

But the diagnosis of AS left Alex in a deep forest without his map. There was no trace of the paths from before: Becoming blind, he wouldn't be able to do his financial calculations at work. Becoming immobile, he would have to abandon the activities he loved. And as for goals of the heart, he was lamenting the end of a relationship with a woman whom he'd wanted a future with.

Like a cold wind through solitary pine trees, questions swirled through my friend's mind: *Am I inadequate? Impossible to love? I feel more alone than ever. Before, I was happy to focus on my career and thought that I was doing well, but now it seems like all my opportunities have passed me by. Could it be that I am irretrievably lost?*

Alex kept a normal routine of working, eating, and sleeping. But a shadow loomed over all of these. He didn't have anyone at work who he truly knew, not enough to share his sorrow with them. Mealtime was exhausting: *If I eat this or that, will it aggravate my symptoms?*

There were new components in his day-to-day routine. One was a regiment of steroids that lowered his inflammation. Another was cryotherapy. Do you remember in the *Star Wars* saga when they froze Han Solo? They did something like that to Alex. He went into a chamber of air that was super-cooled by liquid nitrogen to ease the ache in his muscles.

IT'S IN THOSE MOMENTS OF AFFLICTION WHEN YOU DECIDE what or who you turn to.

Alex told me he came to a crossroads. On the left, he could abandon God. If he took that direction, he'd become a hedonist, grabbing what God, it seemed, wouldn't give him. To the right, he could press into God.

Jesus Christ said:

> Come to me, all who labor and are heavy laden, and I will give you rest. Take my yoke upon you, and learn from me, for I am gentle and lowly in heart, and you will find rest for your souls. (Matthew 11:28–29)

"Heavy laden." Alex could identify with that. But "rest for your souls" was elusive for him. Frankly, he felt a distance between himself and Christ. Well, in that case, the call to "come to me" applied to him. Now, it's not that Alex had turned atheist. No, he'd been a believer his whole life and, as I saw him, a Christian with no facades. But even believers have to come to Jesus. It's like married couples who, even though they are legally married, need to fan the flames.

Alex chose the path that led to Jesus. Come what may, if he had his God, he would be alright. Alex read the Bible more than ever to hear what God wanted to say to him. He also spent a lot of time on his knees. Instead of voicing his complaints, he remembered one by one his reasons to be grateful. My friend explained to me that faith is not about simply adding practices in your life, but rather saturating yourself in the presence of God.

Even so, some days he woke up with hunger pains no food could satisfy. There between the sheets, his spirit groaned inside of him. He suddenly felt like hiding under the covers and diving into the bitterness. That would please his ego for a moment, but it invariably left him depressed. He realized that once again he needed to turn to Christ. Like eating or sleeping, He is sustenance you have to have day-in and day-out.

As for me, I bought a plane ticket. Weeks after the bad news, I was back in Oregon. While there for our friend's wedding, I appointed myself Alex's personal breakfast chef. I got to his house early and let myself in (I still remembered the code to the garage door) with a bag of ingredients—the good stuff.

Later, Alex came down the stairs to see vapor from the boiling water for coffee, to hear sizzling bacon, and to smell stacks of pancakes. If food opens a man's heart, I wanted to put some encouragement in there.

I returned to Morelia, Mexico, and the summer months went by. In November, I spoke to Alex again. We got caught up on jobs, family, and our friends in Portland. The conversation flew all over like a bird, but I wanted to land on how he was holding up with his condition.

"God loves me," responded Alex with complete certainty.

He had always been a sincere person, but I had never heard him talk like this. His voice had momentum, as if his soul was surfing a big wave. Many people shipwreck on the coral reef of their problems, but Alex was gliding right over it.

The next month, I returned to Portland for Christmas and New Year's. We were sitting at Alex's dining room table. On the plate in front of me sat a rosemary-basted chicken leg that had just come out of the oven. On the side were diced zucchini and carrots. The vegetables lay under a blanket of gravy with garlic, celery, and onion. It turned out that Alex had become quite the chef. I told you he was a goal-setter!

Between bites, I asked him about the conviction I had noticed in his voice the previous month. "How are you so sure God loves you?" He explained that in one of his freak-out moments, Alex prayed and God showed up. It was just like this verse:

> Do not be anxious about anything, but in everything by prayer and supplication with thanksgiving let your requests be made known to God. And the peace of God, which surpasses all understanding, will guard your hearts and your minds in Christ Jesus. (Philippians 4:6–7)

He told me about an episode with anxiety after work. Walking in the shadow of the skyscrapers downtown, his cell phone vibrated with an incoming call. The screen read *Ryan Samuelsen*. Alex had not talked with this mutual college friend in seven years. Ryan had been our ministry leader, a gentle but strong man, humble but the most outstanding engineer in his class. If anyone could have spoken on behalf of God, it would have been Ryan. "Alex, I'm here looking at your photo and praying for you. How have you been?"

How could Ryan have known the valley Alex was crossing? Alex had told barely anyone. Various people like Ryan came out of the blue and made contact with Alex. Taking it all together, "I understood it like a hug from God," Alex told me.

During my stay in Portland, I expected ankylosing spondylitis to be the black hole of our attention. That its gravity would affect every conversation and dictate each ingredient in our meals. But it wasn't like that. If it hadn't been for me asking, Alex probably wouldn't have mentioned it. It's not that he had anything to hide; it's just that he had set his gaze on something else. When you listen as Christ says "come to me," you fixate on Him.

OUR PLATES WERE CLEAN IN FRONT OF US, AND OUR GLASSES had only rings of foam left in them. The conversation had also come to its natural end.

"You know what?" Alex said. "God has even changed my personality. I feel more awake to my emotions. When I read the Scriptures, they come to life. I hadn't noticed that in his letters, Paul was effusive, poetic. He had a longing for the people he wrote to. The words of Jesus speak to me like never before."

I'll share one of the passages that has spoken most to Alex recently. I'll say as a way of prologue that when facing death, you don't need good vibes, as though positivity could change your mortality. You need a rock-solid promise. On this, you can anchor your hope. Let's see it:

> Behold! I tell you a mystery. We shall not all sleep, but we shall all be changed, in a moment, in the twinkling of an eye, at the last trumpet. For the trumpet will sound, and the dead will be raised imperishable, and we shall be changed. For this perishable body must put on the imperishable, and this mortal body must put on immortality. When the perishable puts on the imperishable, and the mortal puts on

immortality, then shall come to pass the saying that is written:

"Death is swallowed up in victory."

"O death, where is your victory? O death, where is your sting?"

The sting of death is sin, and the power of sin is the law. But thanks be to God, who gives us the victory through our Lord Jesus Christ.

Therefore, my beloved brothers, be steadfast, immovable, always abounding in the work of the Lord, knowing that in the Lord your labor is not in vain. (1 Corinthians 15:51–58)

THERE ARE TIMES WHEN "TAKE THE LEAP" DOESN'T MEAN jumping from a height, but rather that your ship is sinking and you have to jump toward whatever will save you. Alex discovered that you can let it sink—and your maps with it.

The only thing that has always mattered is the One you turn to: Jesus.

NINETEEN
TO THE ONE WHO OVERCOMES
PERSEVERE TO THE END

When you find out the game you're playing is rigged—the game you practiced for through sweat and tears, the game you played with all your heart—what do you do? Do you run to give them a show? I don't. I walk off the field.

It all started in high school when Mrs. Dowd handed our essays back. One by one, she put them facedown on our desks. As she approached my desk, I could feel her presence. Yes, she was a stocky woman, but I think it was her face. Her expression told us this was a graded composition, and you don't take compositions lightly. Not even her curly brown hair that bounced with her steps could lighten the mood.

But I didn't let myself get intimidated. For me, this was a familiar scenario. Some people are born leaders, others are natural basketball players, and I was born for academia. Multiple choice? Bring it on. Essays? Challenge accepted.

I calmly turned my essay over to see my grade. My jaw dropped. It looked like the scene of a violent crime; with red ink on every line, my assignment had been axed to death. I'd received a D. I never got D's; if I got a B, I would be stressed. It felt like Mrs. Dowd had in fact knifed me.

Was I the only one taken by surprise? I turned my head

subtly, hoping to see the panic-stricken faces of my classmates. Defeat isn't as bitter if you're not the only victim, you know? But I didn't see anyone else looking scared. They looked at their reports like it was any other normal day.

That was my first assignment with Mrs. Dowd, the first of all those that would come in the next four years of my life. It didn't look good. Weeks ago, I had been excited to be signed up for Advanced English, the track that focused on literature and composition. But now I started to question: *Should I change my course schedule so I could be in normal English classes?*

When I brought this worry to my parents, they explained that at the end of four years, I could take an exam called an Advanced Placement test (AP test). If I passed, I would be awarded college credits, which would be worth more than three thousand dollars. I concluded that I could bear with the course load today if I would reap the benefits tomorrow.

FOR MY FOUR YEARS OF HIGH SCHOOL, I LEARNED THE meaning of the word *effort*. My bedroom turned into a jail cell I didn't leave in the afternoons. I typed my reports and literary analyses until my eyes hurt. I often got up at five in the morning to finish them. And I swear, it didn't matter how many times I double-checked the documents for errors, I never got a grade above a B. I wasn't lacking in spelling or word count, but structure and clarity of expression.

It seemed like I was the only one who stumbled under the weight of Advanced English. My friends, also nerds, did well. There were cool kids in the class too. You know them: bigheaded kids, the ones who make fun of how their class-mates are dressed, the ones who smile at the teacher but curse her behind her back. They were definitely not bookworms, but I saw them do well. This confused me: *0 + 0 = 9? What are they doing to get outstanding grades? The universe doesn't work like this!*

Okay, whatever. My conviction was still that doing honest work honored God.

There is a book that even today makes me shudder: *Crime and Punishment* by Fyodor Dostoyevsky. At the end of my junior year of high school, days before summer break, with the warm breeze drifting in through the windows, Mrs. Dowd assigned us this book as summer reading. I think it weighed as much as a cinder block —and it was just about as thick. Anyone who reads it deserves a gold medal, but she was asking us to do a deep analysis of its characters, recurring themes, and literary technique. Our teacher told us not to procrastinate, as the workload would be similar to a part-time job. What crime had I done to warrant this punishment?

I knew I'd never be able to do it. From June to August, I would be working at a summer camp in Maine. At 5:30 in the morning, I'd be waking up to lead the boys: we would be climbing mountains with big packs and zigzagging down rivers in canoes. Our nights would end with campfires. I would only have ninety minutes of downtime each day. For an adventurer, it was the perfect job. For a scholarly critic of Russian novels, it was horrible.

I tried to explain my dilemma to Mrs. Dowd. She listened without a trace of compassion in her eyes. "Fine," she finally said. "If you don't do this project, you can continue in the class, but know that your grade point average at the end of the year won't be higher than a B." Those words hit me like bullets—bullets that tore through more than a paper diploma and my ego; they went right through my future.

Universities accept you and offer you scholarships based on your grade point average. But now I couldn't change lanes; I had to take this class. My only consolation was the AP test. It was on the horizon, and it was this trip's destination.

The summer went by, and I was back in high school for my final year. Soon enough, autumn leaves fell in piles of yellow and red, and the wind swept these leaves down the streets. In like manner, I turned page after page of the required reading for this class. Papers fluttered out of my printer, too. As I wrote more essays, I began to comprehend how to structure my ideas and how to express them clearly.

THIS MAKES ME THINK ABOUT OTHER STRESSED-OUT PEOPLE. In the Roman Empire was a city called Pergamum. I'm not an archeologist, but I read that Pergamum was an advanced city, the Bogotá or Chicago of its time. This was where all the cultured kids sat in hipster cafés writing their blogs with chai lattes. Maybe not. But seriously, though, Pergamum *was* a literary hot spot. It was the birthplace of parchment and home to a massive library.[1]

Strangely enough, the most civilized places sometimes turn out to be the most barbaric. In Pergamum, politics were a bribe and love an orgy. It was there that laws protected the fat cats and exploited the weak. If your prayer to God was "Your will be done on earth," you had a problem. God's will and the emperor's will couldn't be done at the same time. If you chose God's will, your day-to-day consisted of resisting the system.

That's how the Christians in Pergamum lived. Christ spoke to them like this:

> The One who has the sharp two-edged sword says this: "I know where you dwell, where Satan's throne is; and you hold firmly to My name, and did not deny My faith even in the days of Antipas, My witness, My faithful one, who was killed among you, where Satan dwells." (Revelation 2:12–13 NASB)

"Where Satan's throne is"?
If there is anyone in the history of the world who could

claim the game was rigged against them, it would have been the Christian resident in that city.

When cheaters prosper and it seems like everyone else but you is also prospering, it makes you wonder about the effectiveness of your integrity. At least, those who lived in Pergamum wondered about this. Some lost heart and allowed themselves to cheat. They took part in idolatry, sexual immorality, and false teachings.

TWO THOUSAND YEARS AFTER PERGAMUM, BACK IN PORTLAND, my day had come. As serious as if she were speaking to astronauts about to lift off, our teacher explained the procedure for the AP test. We would walk in a single file line to the library. The external coordinator would open an official box that had come from Washington, DC. Each one of us would receive the test in a sealed packet.

The next thing I knew, I sat at a table with the test in front of me. The clock had started. They were watching us. My pencil trembled in my hand. I read the passages, but the words and lines melted until I only saw alphabet soup. I blinked hard. I shot a glance at the clock. I dried the sweat on my forehead. I started reading again. I stole another look at the clock. *Andrew, think!* My minutes ticked away. I didn't know what to write. I moved the pencil and put graphite on the page. Picking words at random from a dictionary might have produced a more coherent composition. This time, I didn't care about the structure of my ideas or their clarity.

"Time!" the coordinated announced.

Pencils on the table. Tests in the envelopes. Envelopes in the box. The box to FedEx.

I buried my foot in the accelerator of my pickup and left the school behind in the smoke of my burning tires. The school day had just begun, and I never skipped classes, but I didn't care anymore. I had to leave that place. My knuckles got white as I choked my steering wheel. After driving a while, I saw a park. I decided to stop there.

I didn't have anywhere particular to go, but I needed to walk—I had to let the screaming out of me. I ambled under the shade of the maple trees that covered the pathway. My mind sped faster than my feet: *How can this be happening? How could all my late nights have been in vain? How could my efforts not have added up to anything?*

The test was absurd. The school system, absurd. Integrity, absurd. Maybe life itself was absurd.

Some of my classmates didn't waste a single thought on Christ. But there they were hanging out with the starters on the team, driving fast cars, kissing beautiful girls, and winning scholarships to spend on the promising thing that was their future.

Suddenly, an idea appeared and looked me in the face. *No more.* I wouldn't be the fool, not anymore. For a lot of kids in the United States, college is the time to reinvent yourself. *So, why not me?* I mused. *From here on out, I'll do it my way.* If honest work didn't pay, I'd take another route. If walking with God only tripped me up, another path would do me good.

I felt like a knot was loosening around my neck. New strength pumped through my veins. I left the shade of the branches and started to cross a soccer field that led toward a hilltop. That would be a good place to inaugurate the new Andrew.

HAVE YOU EVER WANTED TO KNOW WHAT JESUS WOULD SAY TO you? Have you ever wanted His voice to guide you through a crucial moment? What if He wrote you a letter? If your answer is yes, you're in good company. This is precisely what Jesus did for our friends in Pergamum. Let's read the first part here: "The one who has an ear, let him hear what the Spirit says to the churches. To the one who overcomes ..." (Revelation 2:17 NASB).

There is a promise coming for "the one who overcomes." This kind of person fascinates God. If you read chapters 2 and 3 of Revelation, you'll notice He speaks to "the one who overcomes" in every letter to the churches. In total, He says the phrase seven times. It's as if He wanted everyone in the world to know about being an overcomer.

The interesting thing about the phrase is that it doesn't say "to the one who comes." It makes me think of MMA fights or boxing matches on television. In the beginning, the fighters come. They come with their music blasting through the speakers. They come wearing their robes. They come with the backing of their sponsors. They come. But that's not what counts. We watch the fight to see who *overcomes*.

This is what God wants to see as well. He likes to see our boldness and backbone. Look at the words Jesus uses when He writes to the churches: "I know your **deeds** and your **labor** and **perseverance**" (Revelation 2:2), "Be faithful **until death**" (2:10), "you **hold firmly** to My name, and **did not deny** My faith" (2:13), "**hold firmly** until I come" (2:25), "you kept My word of **perseverance**" (3:10), "**hold firmly** to what you have" (3:11) [my emphasis; all from NASB]. This isn't vocabulary for the faint of heart.

In each letter to the churches, Jesus lists different rewards for overcoming. This way, the benefits unfold little by little. They can't fit into one comment or even one letter. We'll unpack a couple of them in a moment.

THE WIND BEGAN TO BLOW WHILE I WALKED UP THE HILL. THE grass swayed about at my ankles. The trees whispered. My steps to the top became heavier, as if I were approaching a portal to another world. Gusts of air wrapped around me flowing over my face like water; my jacket flapped in the current. There are few times in my life when I have felt the presence of God, and what surrounded me that day, I have no doubt, was much more than wind.

Could it be that you're confusing one of life's blows with a knockout? I thought to myself. *Are you going to trade your life with God for one where you call the shots?*

I realized that one day Jesus had also been on a hilltop and had to answer that same question. Would Jesus choose to obey God the Father's will or to do what He Himself wanted?

That He was even on the hill of Golgotha was an outrageous injustice. The pagan leaders had found Him innocent, but they still condemned Him to death. The people who praised Him weeks ago when He'd entered Jerusalem now spat curses. They were tearing open the back of the One who'd healed others. They were murdering the One who'd resurrected others. Everything about this was completely absurd.

After Jesus had been hanging nailed on the cross for hours, the sky turned black at midday, and "he said, 'It is finished,' and he bowed his head and gave up his spirit" (John 19:30).

And then I understood that Jesus persevered until the end. He overcame.

I fell to my knees, tears burning down my cheeks. "It is finished." His suffering was finished. God's holy wrath against sin was finished. That means my separation from God was also finished. On the cross of Calvary, God turned the absurd into the magnificent because Jesus suffered in my place.

I stayed there, surrounded by His presence, praying. There I made my decision: *If I know He made a way for a beautiful ending, I can persevere in the meantime.*

DEAR READER, I KNOW YOU SEE SOME MORE PAGES, AND naturally you know the story doesn't end here. That's how it is when you persevere: there's sweat and tears, but then comes the best part.

We didn't finish the letter to Pergamum, did we? Let's read:

> The one who has an ear, let him hear what the Spirit says to the churches. To the one who overcomes, I will give some of the hidden manna, and I will give him a white stone, and a new name written on the stone which no one knows except the one who receives it. (Revelation 2:17 NASB)

What is manna? That was the same question the Israelites asked while they crossed the wilderness. God was guiding them through a dusty landscape. There weren't any cornfields. There weren't many springs of water. These were ideal conditions to die of exposure. But each morning, the Israelites woke up to find a fine, flaky substance on the ground. They could make bread with it, which tasted like honey-sweetened cookies. They said, "What's this?" or in their language, *"Manna?"*

Now, if every day you got up to see food had miraculously appeared, what would you conclude? That your trip was sustained by random chance? By your genius? Obviously not. You would know something is working in your favor. And not only would you know it, but everyone who hears about it would know it. When the Israelites arrived at their destination, Canaan, they already had a legendary reputation. Properly spoken, their God had a reputation.

I've always read this passage in Revelation thinking manna was a prize for those who make it to the end. But why would you need manna if you've arrived? Today I think it's about following Christ wherever He goes and then in retrospect you'll see what you couldn't see in the moment: it was Him sustaining you all the way.

Hidden manna is only half of Christ's promise in this

verse. He also promises *"a white stone, and a new name written on the stone which no one knows except the one who receives it."*

Before the challenge, you don't know yourself. But when you push yourself beyond what you thought was possible, you discover what you are made of. My friend Alex runs marathons, and when he gets philosophical, he tells me about his experiences. I listen closely to him. But since I don't run, no matter how much I listen to him, my imagination can't comprehend what he experienced. Only Alex knows.

An observer thinks he knows your name. He thinks he knows your biography and the causes of your success. But there are depths to yourself only you can fathom. Jesus invites you to persevere and discover who you truly are.

TWO MONTHS AFTER MY TRAUMATIC AP TEST, I WAS BACK IN the forests of Maine, working at summer camp again. Since the camp was rustic and the cabins didn't even have electricity, it was a big deal when we got mail. At dinnertime, they called me up to get an envelope. I saw the return address, and my stomach turned to stone.

It was my AP test result. I already knew what they'd say. I left the dining hall so nobody would see me get emotional. I closed my eyes and opened the envelope. I got a four. Four points out of a maximum of five—enough to receive college credits.

Years later, I graduated college, and today I have a job that surpasses my teenage dreams. Mrs. Dowd didn't ruin my future after all. If it weren't for her, I wouldn't enjoy writing today. My name is still Andrew, but I'm looking forward to my white stone. I'm sure of this: God is sustaining me through each desert I cross, and I will be an overcomer until I see Him face to face.

EPILOGUE

Dear Reader,

My friends and I are here, thirty feet below you, floating in the river. We're cheering you on to take that step forward into midair. And, yes, the water is fine.

Taking the leap means following Jesus even when you don't know how it will work out, even when it's scary. But in the end, you discover it was no risk after all. Everything you lost turned out to be no comparison to what you gained: God Himself.

The real danger in all this is walking away. It's seeing Jesus, hearing His teachings, but then going your own way.

Can I prove it to you?

And by this we know that we have come to know him, if we keep his commandments. Whoever says "I know him" but does not keep his commandments is a liar, and the truth is not in him, but whoever keeps his word, in him truly the love of God is perfected. By this we may know that we are in him: whoever says he abides in him ought to walk in the same way in which he walked. (1 John 2:3–6)

Did you notice that obedience is directly tied to knowing God and living life with Him? You can't have Him on your terms.

So if obeying God is so important, can I ask you a question? How can you do that if you don't know what He said?

I urge you to open your Bible. Reading is a discipline like lifting weights. It hurts. In the beginning, you won't be able to do it much. But stay with it because you will grow stronger and your comprehension will deepen.

Memorize Scripture. Seriously. Write out a few verses on a notecard, put it in your wallet, and pull it out during the day. My parents had me do this, and let me tell you, the mental effort I made in elementary school has benefited me for decades afterward. Memorize parts of the Bible not so people think you're smart, but to get the one thing you need: the living God.

Learning is much easier to do when you have people who are doing it with you. Do you have friends in your life who love God? If not, find them. At all costs, get and keep this kind of friend. When the time comes to take a risk to obey Jesus, they'll be there to back you up. They might even grab your hand and jump with you.

And when you do this, you'll see what God's intention was all along: not only does He lavish you with His presence, He gives you every good thing. You've read how God made friends out of my enemies, laughter out of my loneliness. You've read how following God's good commands surprised me with adventure.

So now, dear reader, go see for yourself. Take the leap.

Much love to you,

Andrew Moses

ACKNOWLEDGMENTS

Three and a half years in the making, this project felt like pushing a train uphill, both ways, in the snow. Friends, I lived off your encouragement.

Josh, Alex, Brad, Jeff, Claudia, Diego, Said and Daine, Brett, Brian, Hugo, Laurie, Uncle Glenn, Mom, and Dad, you are beautiful and brave. Thank you for letting me share your stories.

Mom, Dad, and Kerri, thank you for cheering me on.

Scarlett Figueroa and Priscila López, you crushed it with the book cover!

Elaini Garfield, your insights were the keys that opened the final locks in this manuscript.

Saraí Rosas, you read this book when it was a rough draft. Very rough. Thank you for going above and beyond to help me make this book and its small group curriculum. You're an incredible partner in ministry!

Diego Colindres, if this book has humor and wonder in its pages, you helped put it there.

Andrés Panasiuk, you invested in a little guy like me! Thank you for helping me navigate the business side of publishing a book.

Ireidis Landaeta, you are a dynamo of volition! A hard-working, promise-keeping editor. Fun fact: this book was originally written in Spanish.

Danielle Dyal, thank you for untangling my sentences.

Shauna Perez, an editor and an encourager. It was a joy to see you exceed my expectations.

JD Kudrick, your proofreading was on point.

Marianie Bedolla, thank you for answering a hundred text messages about tricky words I didn't know how to translate. I'm honored to have you on my team.

Julio Favela, this book found its title from your efforts. Thank you!

Grant Williams, Juan Peralta, Felipe Reyna, and so many other friends, you listened to these chapters way before they were ready to share.

Saraí, Estefa, Heber, Adriel, Abraham, Laura, Natán, Samara, Camila, Scarlett, Diego, Daniela, Hugo, Horte, and Mon: Lectores Beta, this book has your fingerprints all over it.

To everyone who I've been telling about this book over the years, thanks for waiting. I hope it was well worth it.

SOURCES CITED

If Your Eye Causes You to Sin

1. Eric Metaxas, *Bonhoeffer: Pastor, Martyr, Prophet, Spy* (Nashville: Thomas Nelson, 2015).

2. "How Porn Changes the Brain," Fight the New Drug, August 23, 2017, https://fightthenewdrug.org/how-porn-changes-the-brain/.

3. "Why Consuming Porn Is an Escalating Behavior," Fight the New Drug, August 23, 2017, https://fightthenewdrug.org/why-consuming-porn-is-an-escalating-behavior/.

Your Inner World

1. Viktor E. Frankl, *Man's Search for Meaning* (Boston: Beacon Press, 2006).

Let Your Yes Be Yes

1. Mariano José de Larra, "Vuelva Usted Mañana," *El Pobrecito Hablador*, January 1833, http://www.cervantesvirtual.-

com/obra-visor/vuelva-usted-manana--0/html/ff7a5caa-82b1-11df-acc7-002185ce6064_2.html.

2. Thomas Nagel, "The Absurd," *The Journal of Philosophy*, Vol. 68, No. 20 (Oct. 21, 1971): 716–727.

When You Stumble Upon Treasure

1. Graeme Goldsworthy, *Gospel and Kingdom* (Milton Keynes, England: Paternoster Press, 2012).

Power and Authority

1. Dirección General de Planeación, Programación y Estadística, "Principales Cifras del Sistema Educativo Nacional 2018–2019" (Ciudad de México, México: Primera Edición, 2019).

2. Miguel Delgado Helleseter, "English Skills and Wages in a Non-English Speaking Country: Findings from Online Advertisements in Mexico," *Education First: EF English Proficiency Index* (Miami Beach, Florida: Education First, 2013).

To the One Who Overcomes

1. *Encyclopaedia Britannica Online*, s.v. "The History of Libraries: The Ancient World—Pergamum," accessed April 2, 2021, https://www.britannica.com/topic/library/The-history-of-libraries#ref62576.

CAN YOU HELP?

Were you encouraged by reading this book? Would you like this message of risk-taking faith to get to more people? If so, you can help! Your reviews on bookselling platforms like amazon.com and review sites like goodreads.com are vital to making *Take The Leap* visible in the online marketplace.

Feel free to grab one of these ideas to get you started:
How did your thinking change?
Have you decided to do something based on
what you read?
What was your favorite part?
Which other book is *Take the Leap* similar to?
What is Andrew's writing style like?

Scan this to leave a review at Amazon!

CONNECT WITH ANDREW

I'd love to hear from you!

A teacher and a storyteller at heart, I'm available to speak at your church, summer camp, or event.

To catch my latest thoughts and stories, I blog and send newsletters out of www.andrewmoseswrites.com.

Email: andrew@andrewmoseswrites.com.

Instagram: @andrewmoseswrites.

Facebook: fb.me/andrewmosesauthor

Made in the USA
Columbia, SC
24 November 2021

49648037R00105